Battered But Not Broken

Battered But Not Broken

Help for Abused Wives and Their Church Families

Patricia Riddle Gaddis

Judson Press ® Valley Forge

Battered But Not Broken: Help for Abused Wives
and Their Church Families
© 1996 Judson Press, Valley Forge, PA 19482-0851

Unless otherwise noted, Bible quotations in this volume are from The *Good News Bible,* the Bible in Today's English Version. Copyright © American Bible Society, 1976. Used by permission. Other quotations are from HOLY BIBLE: *New International Version,* copyright © 1973, 1978, 1984. Used by permission of Zondervan Bible Publishers.

Library of Congress Cataloging-in-Publication Data

Gaddis, Patricia Riddle.
    Battered but not broken : help for abused wives and their church families / Patricia Riddle Gaddis.
        p. cm.
    Includes bibliographical references.
    ISBN 0-8170-1241-9 (pbk.)
    1. Church work with abused women. I. Title.
BV4445.5.G33 1996
    261.8'3315553—dc2095-46617

Printed in the U.S.A.

96 97 98 99 00 01 02 03   8 7 6 5 4 3 2 1

To my son, Shawn; my dear mother;
and Edward and Therese

In memory of Betsy Pressley,
murdered by her husband on February 14, 1993

"May Perpetual Light shine upon her..."

Contents

Acknowledgments

It takes numerous people in addition to the author to write a book. With that in mind, I would like to thank my coworkers Margaret Sluder, Lisa Cloyd, and Dr. Harry Manes for their invaluable professional insights on the problem of abuse. Thanks also to Debra L. and Donna P. for their courage to step forward and assist battered women; to my brother, Bob, for responding so enthusiastically to my ideas; and to Sandra Glass of U.N.C.A., whose computer wizardry allowed me to meet necessary deadlines.

I am grateful for my friends Eleanor Hazell, Joan Garland, Barbara and David Love, Charles and Jenni Band, Gertrude Badurski, Deb and Phil Lowery, and my goddaughters, Rebecca and Emily, who all stood supportively at my side during my mother's illness. Without their friendship I probably could not have completed the manuscript. My love for them is deep and abiding.

Most of all I am grateful to my son, Shawn, who shared his historical expertise and gave up his office and personal word processor, largely without complaint, during the long weeks I was closeted away with my work.

Introduction

My God, my God, why have you abandoned me?
I have cried desperately for help,
   but still it does not come.
During the day I call to you, my God,
   but you do not answer;
I call at night,
   but get no rest.
My strength is gone,
   gone like water spilled on the ground.
All my bones are out of joint;
   My heart is like melted wax.
My throat is dry as dust,
   and my tongue sticks to the roof of my mouth.
You have left me for dead in the dust.

—Psalm 22:1-2,14-15

She Remembers

White lace and candles.
Bridesmaids posed and waiting
for the promises strung like diamonds
on a necklace of dreams.
Now, in the stillness of blood and tears
there is a listening shadow.
Faded image of a prince that
would not bow to light.

—Patricia Riddle Gaddis

Each day we hear or read stories of women being battered, even murdered, by their husbands or boyfriends. Domestic violence, also known as partner abuse, spouse abuse, or battering, is pervasive in our society, and women are consistently reported to be the primary victims. It occurs among all sectors of society and crosses all socioeconomic boundaries, religious beliefs, educational levels, and ethnic backgrounds. Domestic violence affects our lives, our homes, our communities, and perhaps, most importantly, our spiritual development.

Domestic violence is, simply put, the mistreatment of one family member by another. It includes kicking, slapping, punching, choking, the use of weapons, and murder. It is the pattern of behavior that establishes control and power over another person through fear and intimidation, often including the threat or use of violence. Studies indicate that battering escalates over a period of time, beginning with behaviors like threats, destroying property, name calling, and then escalating to pushing, slapping, and life-threatening assaults. Violence against women and children has been approved for many centuries by both civil and religious authorities.

Religion or faith in God does not prevent men from battering. In fact, it is estimated that one out of four members of the faith community is a victim/survivor of domestic violence, yet the church still most often fails to assist the victim of abuse and, in many cases, worsens the problem by blaming the victim.

In my work as shelter program coordinator and advocacy counselor for a domestic violence agency, each day I assist women who have been choked, stabbed, thrown through glass doors, pushed from moving vehicles, held at gunpoint for hours, and beaten beyond recognition. Most of them have had body, mind, and spirit beaten down to practically nothing. Because I live in the "Bible-belt" region of the South, a great many of these women are Christians, married to men who are actively involved in the faith community. In the South, one's Christianity is as big a part of one's heritage as fried chicken and grits. Since the South is probably the most culturally settled region in the United States, most southerners are able to trace their families as far back as the Revolution. It is rare for human service providers in the South to come across an individual who professes to be anything other than a Christian.

Frequently these abused women are advised by their pastors to "pray harder" and "make a greater effort at becoming a better wife," as if the abuse were something the victim deserved or could fully control. Unfortunately, this type of counsel serves to further victimize the woman in crisis. It chips away at her spiritual identity and self-esteem, and at the same time fosters self-blame, which in no way serves to resolve or alleviate the danger that she faces.

While numerous members of the faith community advise the battered woman to "submit" and "pray harder for change within the marital relationship," there seems to be a tendency to also blame the battered woman when she returns to her abusive spouse. One minister of a mainline denomination who has been known to advise battered women to "submit and pray for a miracle" recently told me that he could not understand why battered women "go back for more." A paradoxical blaming pattern among many within the faith community holds the woman responsible for the violence yet harshly judges her for going back to her partner after an escape!

Through my work I have become aware that violence against women is one of the most pressing social problems of our time. Although many churches still view the problem of domestic violence as a private matter, there is nothing private about the fact that domestic violence is the leading cause of injury to women between the ages of fifteen and forty-four. It is more common than automobile accidents, muggings, and rapes combined. Every year, domestic violence results in more than one hundred thousand days of hospitalizations, more than thirty thousand emergency-room visits, and almost forty thousand visits to a physician.[1] And although official estimates of domestic violence originate from the FBI, law enforcement agencies, and hospitals, we must take into consideration the fact that battered women also report domestic violence to friends, clergy, private physicians, and nurses who are not included in national crime surveys. In their 1992 study, Evan Stark and Anne Flitcraft found that out of one million women who sought medical treatment for injuries sustained by husbands and boyfriends, doctors correctly identified the injuries as a result of battering only 4 percent of the time.[2] According to the *Journal of the American*

Medical Association (1990), up to 35 percent of the women who visit emergency rooms are there for injuries related to ongoing abuse.[3]

Child abuse and domestic violence go hand in hand and cannot be separated. Yet for years, judges have granted custody and visitation rights to abusive men, as if a man who abuses his wife would not hurt the children. Studies show that up to 70 percent of men who abuse their female partners also abuse their children.[4] Extensive research shows that in homes where domestic violence occurs, children are abused at a rate 1,500 percent higher than the national average. In addition, 62 percent of sons over the age of fourteen were injured when attempting to protect their mothers from attacks by abusive male partners. Further, many abusive men inadvertently injure children while throwing furniture or other household objects at their female partners, and the youngest children sustain the most serious injuries, such as concussions and broken shoulders and ribs.[5] Even before birth, some children's lives are threatened by abuse. In their 1992 study, Stark and Flitcraft found that from 15 to 25 percent of pregnant women are battered.[6] In another study it was found that out of twelve hundred white, Latina, and African American pregnant women, one in six reported physical abuse during pregnancy.[7]

Despite the common perception that most battered women do not leave their abusive situations, in reality up to 50 percent of all homeless women and children in this country are fleeing from domestic violence. But those who do not leave have their reasons. Statistics reveal, for instance, that women who leave their batterers are at a 75 percent greater risk of being killed by their abusers than those who stay; fleeing can often incite the rage of the abuser to a murderous level. Also, space limitations in shelter programs mean that many who try to escape cannot find a place to go; for every woman accepted into a battered woman's shelter, two women and her children are turned away. Women have many other individual reasons to remain with or go back to an abusive partner.

While the focus is on the victim, we need also to ask of the abuser: Why does he beat her, and why do we as a society condone abusive behavior? (I intentionally use the pronoun *he* to refer to the abuser, for contrary to the belief that domestic violence works both ways, in 95 percent of all domestic violence assaults, crimes are committed by men against women. [8])

If you are a member of the clergy, you are in an ideal position to speak out against domestic violence from the pulpit and throughout the faith community. An overwhelming number of battered women have strong spiritual convictions regarding marriage, and they are drawn to church for comfort and spiritual counsel. This is where your religious training can be either a major help or a terrible hindrance to the woman in crisis. I hope that this book will help you gain the understanding and basic tools you need to help women who are being battered by their partners.

If you are a battered woman and happen to find "your story" in these pages, you can take solace in the fact that you are not alone. The stories in this book are all true, but names and other identifying details have been changed to protect the privacy of those who participated in my research. Stories of domestic violence are not unique—yet this does not mean that your story is unimportant! To get help, call the domestic violence help line in your area (see Appendix A) and talk to a counselor. Find out what your options are, and then begin a new life for yourself—because beyond the brokenness you can find wholeness and peace.

NOTES

1. *The Interchange for Mental Health Professionals*, December 1993, 9.

2. Evan Stark and Anne Flitcraft, *Medical Therapy as Repression: The Case of the Battered Woman*, 1992.

3. From *Journal of the American Medical Association*, as reported in a fact sheet of the National Coalition Against Domestic Violence (NCADV).

4. From Bowker, Arbitell, and McFerron, "On the Relationship between Wife Beating and Child Abuse," *Feminist Perspectives on Wife Abuse*, Kersti, Yllo and Michelle Bogard, eds., Focus Edition Series (Newbury Park, Calif.: Sage Publications, Inc., 1988), as reported in an NCADV fact sheet.

5. From Maria Roy, *Children in the Crossfire,* 1988, as reported in an NCADV fact sheet.

6. From Stark and Flitcraft, 1992, as reported in an NCADV fact sheet.

7. J. McFarlane, "Abuse During Pregnancy: A Cross-Cultural Study of

Frequency and Severity of Injuries," 1991, as reported in an NCADV fact sheet.

8. "Report to the Nation on Crime and Justice," Bureau of Justice Statistics, 1983. According to a Senate Judiciary Report, women are six times more likely than men to be victims of violent assault in intimate relationships. In 1991, more than ninety women were murdered every week; nine out of ten were murdered by men. (Senate Judiciary Committee Report—"Violence against Women: A Week in the Life of America," October 1992, as reported in an NCADV fact sheet.)

My heart is in anguish within me;
   the terrors of death assail me.
Fear and trembling have beset me;
   horror has overwhelmed me.
I said, "Oh, that I had the wings of a dove!
   I would fly away and be at rest—
I would flee far away
and stay in the desert;
I would hurry to my place of shelter,
   far from the tempest and storm."

If an enemy were insulting me,
   I could endure it;
if a foe were raising himself against me,
   I could hide from him.
But it is you, a man like myself,
   my companion, my close friend,
with whom I once enjoyed sweet fellowship
   as we walked with the throng at the house of God.

My companion attacks his friends;
   he violates his covenant.

           —Psalm 55:5-8,12-14,20, NIV

CHAPTER ONE

Kimberly's Story

One of my first clients was a woman whom I will call Kimberly. She was thirty-four and had beautiful, thick, auburn hair, arranged in a pageboy style, and a flawless complexion. The day she came to the clinic she wore a stunning emerald suit, perfectly accented with gold jewelry. If I had seen her in a restaurant or airport, I would have thought she was a high-powered business executive on her way to an important meeting. But in reality, she was on her way to see the dentist.

Her husband, Bob, had smashed his fist into her face several times the evening before, blackening her eye and breaking a tooth. Dark glasses concealed her swollen eye, and heavy makeup covered the bruises around her mouth and jaw. Her right hand was neatly wrapped in white gauze. Bob had angrily slammed the front door on her fingers as she was trying to escape his rage. The next morning he felt guilty and had given her a generous amount of cash to pay for her medical care. She had driven all the way from Asheville just to see a dentist. Why? Because her husband was a prominent "man about town," and driving thirty-five miles west to my small mountain county gave her anonymity.

Like most battered women, Kimberly was suffering from the side effects of low self-esteem. As impeccably dressed as she was, her shoulders were slightly bent, and many of her expressions were prefaced with "I'm sorry." Bob held several key leadership roles in the church, and Kimberly felt certain that God no longer cared about her. In fact, she believed that she was actually being punished for something, although she couldn't quite figure out what she had done to deserve the almost constant physical and emotional abuse from her husband. She felt helpless, hopeless, and very much alone.

Kimberly and Bob had met at a tennis match in college. They dated one another on and off for a few weeks, and then Bob began sending her flowers and poetic love notes. Within a short time he had presented her with a stunning one-carat-diamond engagement ring. Kimberly was flattered but did not accept his proposal because she wanted to complete her education before making a serious commitment. A bright woman, she had been inducted into the prestigious Phi Beta Kappa and had set some goals for her life.

Bob sulked for a short while and then began stalking her, although at the time Kimberly did not know that it was stalking. She just knew that he seemed to appear wherever she happened to be. If she went out to the movies with her girlfriends, Bob appeared. When she dated other guys, he showed up at the restaurants where they dined. He left love notes with the college dorm mother and sent so many flowers that her room smelled like a florist's. Kimberly was young and did not understand the difference between admiration and pathological jealousy. Bob was charming and came from an incredibly wealthy family. All of her friends thought she was crazy for not allowing the relationship to continue, for Bob was truly a "Prince Charming"—right down to his white Mercedes.

So at last, under peer pressure, Kimberly gave in and began dating Bob once more. His jealousy escalated. He no longer allowed her to go places with her friends because he "loved her" so much that he didn't want her out of his sight. He gave her another engagement ring, a two-carat diamond this time, and they began to plan an elaborate wedding. He "allowed" her to complete her undergraduate studies but insisted that she drop the idea of pursuing a master's degree, since his wife would never need to work outside the home. Her role was to accompany him to social gatherings and church functions, and, in return, she would never be without all of the luxuries that money could buy.

The wedding was a grand ceremony with ten bridesmaids, followed by a seated dinner reception for several hundred guests. In the darker moments of her life, she would always reserve a special place in her memory for that perfect evening when she and

Bob, surrounded by smiling faces, champagne, and sculptured ice baskets filled with fresh flowers, waltzed like Cinderella and Prince Charming to the music played by a twelve-piece orchestra that had been flown into town just for them.

The beatings began shortly after a two-week honeymoon to Hawaii. They had temporarily settled into a cozy but luxurious condominium near the university where Bob was finishing his graduate studies. They lived on a generous monthly allowance from Bob's parents. As soon as Bob completed his graduate program, he would go to work for his father's firm and make a six-figure salary. Kimberly's culinary repertoire contained only two or three main courses, but she was always trying out new recipes from the numerous cookbooks that Bob's mother had given her. One evening she had prepared a chicken casserole for dinner and had even baked a pineapple upside-down cake. They were about halfway through the meal when Bob let out a howl and held up a small piece of chicken bone he had bitten into. In a flash, Bob was on his feet, throwing the glass casserole dish against the wall and turning over the dining-room table, scattering silverware and glasses everywhere. In shock and panic, Kimberly made a mad dash for the front door, but before she could escape, he caught her by the arm and screamed, "You stupid bitch! Can't you do *anything* right?"

The shock of his fist against her face made her gasp with pain and horror. Her Prince Charming had turned into a monster right before her eyes. As he drove his fists into her, she heard the cracking of her own bones and knew that her ribs had snapped. Falling to the floor, she tried shielding her face with her hands, but he only kicked her arms away and continued to beat her without mercy until she passed out. When she came to, she knew that she had been hurt very badly. Stabs of pain shot through her entire body, and with every breath she took she felt that he must have cracked most of her ribs. A twitch of her finger warned that her arm had been broken, and blinking her eyes made her feel as though her head might split wide open.

She groaned, and within seconds Bob was kneeling at her side, covering her bloody face with a cold cloth. He was crying uncontrollably and begging her forgiveness. Kimberly felt the presence of a second person in the room. And as Bob continued to whimper in sorrow over what he had done, this Heavenly Presence seemed to saturate her and comfort her in a way that she had experienced only once before in her life, when she was a little girl and had been injured in a nearly fatal bike accident. As she lay there, helpless, broken, and unable to move, she "heard" this Presence, whom she identified as the Lord Jesus, telling her to leave Bob before it was too late. What has happened to me? she wondered. I once had so many goals in my life. I had gifts that I was using to help others. But I stopped praying for guidance when I met Bob. I replaced that part of my life with delusions of grandeur.

As Bob carried her into the emergency room of a hospital in a neighboring town, the nurses on duty thought she had been in an automobile accident. Kimberly heard Bob tell them that she had fallen down a flight of stairs. She felt certain that the doctor on call knew better, and she wanted to tell him the truth. But the words would not come out of her mouth, and Bob refused to leave her side. In retrospect, Kimberly realized that he remained close at hand to prevent her from revealing that he was the perpetrator.

An orthopedic specialist was called in to set the broken bones in her arm, and when he asked her if she had any questions, she started to cry uncontrollably. A nurse appeared from behind the white curtain, abruptly pushing up her sleeve and jabbing her with a needle. As she felt herself floating off into a blanket of darkness, she heard the doctor giving Bob instructions on how to take care of her. What a cruel joke, Kimberly thought, as she felt herself slipping into a deep sleep. The doctor was actually giving her assailant instructions on how to take care of his victim.

For two months, a nurse came in every day to care for Kimberly. Bob hired a full-time housekeeper to cook all of the meals and clean the house. "He is a perfectionist," Kimberly instructed. "He likes the dishes arranged in a certain order, with the cup handles all facing the same direction. And canned foods must be stacked so that he can see exactly what is in the cupboard, with two cans on the bottom and one can on top in a triangle. All of the towels have to be folded military fashion, and there have to be fresh hand towels hanging in the bathroom at all times."

During her recovery period, Bob treated Kimberly with the greatest respect, bringing home fresh flowers every day and showering her with little love poems that proclaimed his husbandly devotion. Kimberly tried to bring up the issue of the beating with Bob, hoping that they could somehow work the matter out, but Bob would swiftly change the subject. At last, Kimberly decided that his rage was just an isolated incident and would never happen again. She convinced herself that he was under tremendous pressure in graduate school—and made a vow never to serve Bob chicken casserole again.

For almost a year everything went fine. Bob successfully completed his master's program and went to work in his father's firm. They moved into a lovely home, located in the best section of town, and became members of the church. Bob said that going to church would be good for their marriage *and* his business. Kimberly had been raised in the church and was hopeful that their active involvement would serve to strengthen their marriage.

Then, one evening soon after their move, Bob came home from work enraged because his father had called him down about the manner in which he had handled a business transaction. Kimberly tried to calm him down, but the more she attempted to soothe his anger, the more violent he became, slamming doors and using foul language. Then he discovered that Kimberly had not picked up his suit from the cleaners. "How could you be so stupid?" he asked, jerking her up by the collar and slapping her back and forth across the face. "Look outside," he screamed, dragging her over to the window and pressing her face against the glass. "I gave you a brand new car to drive, and yet you can't even go downtown to pick up my suit!" Bob continued to rant and rave, physically abusing her until at last she managed to break away and lock herself in the guest room. There she quickly dialed 911, and when the doorbell rang ten minutes later, Bob stopped banging on the guest room door long enough to go downstairs and answer, all the while thinking that it was his father coming to apologize. Instead, he was shocked to see two police officers asking if they could come in. Although he tried to convince the officers that nothing was wrong, they insisted on looking around, stating that they had received a call from a woman who was crying and said she was being beaten.

When Kimberly heard them downstairs talking to Bob, she immediately began screaming for their help because she knew that once they were gone, Bob would break down the bedroom door and finish her off. When the police officers saw her bruised face and arms, they arrested Bob on the spot and urged Kimberly to take out a warrant against her husband. Although Bob begged her not to do it, she went ahead and pressed charges. Bob spent the night in jail.

While Bob's parents hired an expensive lawyer for their son, Kimberly could not afford legal counsel because all of their money was in Bob's name. Bob had arranged a charge account with one of the grocery stores in town so that when Kimberly went shopping for food, the bill, along with the cash register receipt, was sent to Bob's business. If Kimberly needed clothing, Bob would go with her or send his secretary along to pay the bill. Kimberly could not buy anything without Bob's approval, and of course there was no way that Bob would approve the money for her to hire an attorney.

Bob's mother took Kimberly aside and demanded that she drop the charges. At the same time his mother advised her to "go along with Bob's temper" and avoid "setting him off." Kimberly had just discovered that she was pregnant, and, not knowing what else to do, she dropped the charges and took him back. Bob did not beat Kimberly while she was carrying his child, which is highly unusual. During the course of her pregnancy, they planned an elaborate nursery and purchased expensive baby furniture. They attended Lamaze classes together, and Bob was a willing coach throughout the delivery of his son. Kimberly felt certain that all Bob needed was more love and security; having a family of his own was the perfect cure for his pathological jealousy and obsession.

But when their baby was four months old, the violence began again. This time, Bob accused her of spending too much time with the child. According to Bob, Kimberly was deliberately ignoring him.

In the years to follow, Bob dislocated Kimberly's shoulder three times, blackened her eyes on too many occasions to recall, and accused her of having affairs with everyone from the preacher to the paper boy. After each beating, he would beg her forgiveness. After each beating, she forgave him, and a "honeymoon" would immediately follow. During this honeymoon phase, he would call her up and have her meet him in town for romantic lunches. She would sometimes receive singing telegrams proclaiming his love for her. During this time period, they would communicate better than ever before. Kimberly would always be filled with hope during this phase because she would feel as though she had her "Prince Charming" back. But after each romantic interlude, the clock would strike twelve and she would find herself back at the hospital emergency room, getting her lip sewn up or having a broken bone set.

After several years of living this way, Kimberly took out a criminal assault warrant. Bob begged her to drop charges, and Kimberly countered with an ultimatum: Bob would have to get counseling, or she would take their child and leave him for good. He agreed to see their pastor for counseling, and she dropped the charges.

But in their counseling sessions, their pastor avoided the issue of the violence that was so prominent in the relationship. Instead, he focused on their roles as husband and wife and told Kimberly to "submit" to her husband in all things and not do anything that might "set him off." He told her that she was undoubtedly expecting too much from her husband. At no time did the pastor tell Bob to submit to his wife and love her as Christ loved the church. Nor did he take Kimberly aside and advise her to seek assistance from a domestic violence program. And while Bob's violent behavior clearly warranted a spiritual reprimand, he was neither asked to step down from any of his leadership roles within the church nor referred to a batterer's treatment program. In short, the pastor set this couple up for future violence as he sanctioned Bob's behavior by indicating that Kimberly was somehow responsible for her husband's violence. As a result, Kimberly went away empty, feeling as though God did not care for her feelings.

What Should Kimberly Do?

It is not uncommon for Christian women who are battered to remain with an abusive partner on grounds of scriptural submission. That reasoning was expressed by Kimberly when, removing her dark glasses to reveal a bruised and swollen eye, she asked, "What would *you* do? I truly hate him for hurting me like this, but what if I really *do* burn in hell for breaking up my marriage? And I ask you, could hell be any worse than having to live like *this*?"

Would Kimberly's escape from a violent relationship make *her* responsible for the breakup of her marriage? I don't think so! In fact, my understanding of Paul's teaching on submission actually releases a woman from a violent spouse. Paul clearly states that men are to love their wives as Christ loved the church and gave his life for her (Ephesians 5:25) and that men are to love their wives as they love their own bodies (Ephesians 5:28). One might reasonably conclude from this text that if a man loves his wife as much as Christ loved the church, then he would be willing to die for her, not try to take life from her! Marriage vows were never intended to chain partners into unhealthy and violent relationships. The image of marriage given to us in the Bible is actually that of Jesus giving himself for the church. So when pastors or well-intentioned Christian friends tell a woman to submit to an abusive spouse, they are ignoring God's image of what marriage is to be and are sending a clear-cut message to the world that abuse is acceptable in the eyes of God. Yet as Christians we know that nothing could be further from the truth.

In addition, when abusers such as Bob are allowed to hold leadership roles within the church, violence is in effect upheld as an acceptable Christian practice. Jesus said to the church in Laodicea, "I know what you have done; I know that you are neither cold nor hot. How I wish you were either one or the other! But because you are lukewarm, neither hot nor cold, I am going to spit you out of my mouth" (Revelation 3:15-16). In my opinion, taking a lukewarm position on the issue of domestic violence weakens a congregation. No matter how outwardly prosperous a church may appear, if the pastor and leaders tolerate wife beating, they will not be able to go forward spiritually and experience the full blessings of God. Maintaining a lukewarm position on domestic violence is also dangerous for society in general, for it fosters family violence that spills out onto the streets in the form of street crime and gangs.

Although isolated, Kimberly did reach out for help from various places, mainly the medical profession and her church. No one gave her a referral to a battered women's shelter, however. The attending physicians and nurses at the various hospitals where Kimberly received treatment did not question her about the mysterious fractures and bruises or request that her husband leave the room so that she could speak with medical personnel freely. When Kimberly attempted to seek help from her pastor, he avoided the issue of violence in the marriage instead of addressing it directly with the expansive love of God through Christ. He did not meet with each spouse separately, nor did he remove Bob from his leadership responsibilities in the church.

Despite this lack of support, Kimberly eventually managed to leave Bob and begin a new life for herself. There were several steps in the process that eventually enabled her to escape. First, she began to build a solid, long-term getaway plan that would enable her to avoid having to go back to Bob. This plan included opening up a small savings account of her own, which was difficult in light of the fact that Bob monitored all of their money transactions. She had two sources of income that she could hide in this account. One was to sell some of her most expensive clothing at local consignment shops, and the income from that added up to a generous sum over a period of six to eight months. She also took a temporary job in the church nursery. Bob protested at first, but Kimberly told him that she would like to use the money for Christmas shopping. He reluctantly allowed her to keep the money, which she placed in her secret bank account.

Kimberly continued to drive over to my office to talk to me about her escape plan, and during each visit we would go over the details which she had written in code in her planner so that Bob would not understand if he should happen to read it. Her plan included going to stay with her sister in another state until she could find work. I knew Kimberly could find employment without too much difficulty because she was highly intelligent and had a college degree. Every few weeks she would send to her sister's house a box of clothing and other items that she wanted to keep. She had calculated that the cost of sending by UPS was "cheaper than a moving van and less for me to take along."

Kimberly also met other women through our agency who had escaped abusive situations and were living a life free from violence. This strengthened her resolve to officially end her relationship with Bob. I use the word "officially" because Kimberly had often stated that her marriage to Bob had ended when be began physically abusing her shortly after their wedding.

Kimberly made her escape just four days before Christmas. Bob came in from the office one evening and demanded to see the money that she had been saving from her job. She didn't want to tell him about her own savings account and told him that she had hidden it in her locker at the church. Bob shoved her against the wall and began choking her, telling her what a stupid idiot she was for leaving the money there instead of putting it in the bank. Later, Kimberly told me that she believed Bob sensed something different about her; he had been questioning her more frequently regarding her trips to the dentist and her job at the church.

Finally, Bob stormed out of the house, telling her he was going over to the church to check her locker. As his car sped away into the night, Kimberly hurriedly packed a bag and got their small son into the car. Bob had been in such a rage that he had forgotten to take her car keys. She stopped only once on her way out of town and that was at the bank's automated teller machine to withdraw all of the money she had saved (a little over three thousand dollars). She headed for her sister's house and called me the next day. The only part of her original plan that hadn't worked out was that she was going to leave a day later, after she had received her last paycheck.

The courage to go forward on this journey came ultimately from the memory of Christ's presence on the first night that Bob battered her, combined with the realization that she was not alone, that other women—millions, in fact—were living the same isolated existence. Perhaps if Kimberly had received the necessary support from her church she would have escaped the violence much sooner. But when she finally did find the support she needed, she was able to break the cycle of violence without becoming a statistic on the long list of victims who are murdered daily by an abusive partner.

CHAPTER TWO

Characteristics of the Battered Woman

What kind of woman is battered? Contrary to what some would like to believe, there is not a "typical" woman who will be battered. Battered women come from all types of cultural, racial, economic, and religious backgrounds. The greatest risk factor for being battered seems to be that of being born female. According to the National Coalition Against Domestic Violence, it is estimated that over 50 percent of all women will experience violence in an intimate relationship, and for 24 to 30 percent of those women, the abuse will be ongoing.[1] Furthermore, injuries that battered women receive are at least as serious as injuries suffered in 90 percent of violent felony crimes, yet under state laws, battering cases are almost always classified as misdemeanors.[2]

There are, however, some typical behaviors and feelings that are apt to develop and be exhibited by women who are trapped in an abusive relationship. The battered woman:

- Is often unaware that a crime has been committed against her.
- Is economically dependent on her partner. If she is allowed to work, her partner controls what she spends.
- Fears losing custody of the children. The abusive partner tells her that he will press charges against her for abandonment.
- Fears that her abuser may kidnap the children and she will never see them again.
- Is insecure about being on her own, mainly due to a lack of self-esteem.

- Fears that divorce may not be considered an acceptable option by her church.
- Often has tremendous fear regarding life changes.
- Lacks alternative housing and job skills.
- Hopes that her abuser will change.
- Fears retaliation.
- Is not totally convinced of her right to be free from violence.
- Believes that the violence is at least partially her fault and that she can stop it—so she tries numerous ways of relating to her abuser when he is angry, yet none seem to work.
- Does not want the relationship to end; just wants the violence to stop.

Identifying the Battered Woman

Although a woman may not openly say anything about the abuse she is suffering, here are some signs to watch for:

- She bears numerous unexplained bruises.
- She has vague excuses and hard-to-believe explanations for physical injuries.
- She has few or no friends.
- She has to hang up suddenly when you talk with her on the telephone.
- She must ask permission from her husband to go shopping or out with her girlfriends.
- Her husband or partner calls frequently at her workplace.
- She often appears sad, perhaps for several weeks, and then her demeanor temporarily improves (during this time, she may receive flowers at work from her husband or partner); soon she reverts to appearing sad again.
- During her periods of sadness, she will not tell anyone what is wrong. She often wears long sleeves and looks as though she has been crying.
- She does not join in activities.
- She doesn't stay around after work or church to socialize if her husband or partner is not with her but hurries home instead.
- She has frequent mood changes.

- She is often jittery and on edge.
- She will not allow you to visit her at home.

Be alert for the above characteristics, and if you suspect abuse, diplomatically ask her if she would like to talk to you. Of course, everyone has mood changes from time to time, and all of us may exhibit one or two of these characteristics on occasion. But if you see a pattern developing, then it is important that you make yourself available to her and let her know that you care. This might be successfully accomplished by calling her from time to time and chatting about things that are going on in the church; you could then invite her to go with you to activities that interest her and ones in which she could get involved. To try to help a battered woman overcome her feelings of isolation, you might steer the conversation to whatever problem you happen to be trying to overcome in your own life (without getting too personal). This might have the effect of giving a woman in crisis the courage to open up—if not to you, then maybe to someone else.

A Word about Codependency

Because the woman in crisis survives by being constantly attentive to her abuser's behavior, many counselors label battered women "codependent." A well-intentioned counselor, especially in the drug and alcohol field, will often challenge a battered woman to focus on what she should do to change herself and her dysfunctional family unit. I believe that this label of "codependency," when used to define battered women, serves only to wrongly reprimand the victim. Battered women in fact learn certain survival behaviors that keep them alive. Some of these actions are apt to include constant care giving—making certain that everything—food, housekeeping, and so on—is absolutely "perfect" and the way the batterer likes it. They might include isolating herself from family and friends, as well as an almost total loss of self-esteem.

While the above may appear to be codependent, they are, in fact, important adjustments to her violent environment that help her to survive and avoid injury. The codependency label wrongly reinforces the idea that the beatings are primarily her fault and that, if only she could change, her batterer would stop beating her. She may in fact need counseling to improve her self-esteem, deal with her inflicted trauma, and make some decisions about what to do, but she is not to blame for her partner's violent actions against her.

The Hazelden Family Center in Minnesota has denounced the codependency label for battered women in an article entitled "Behind the Veil of Silence."[3] The article reads as follows:

> Chemical dependency treatment providers need to be aware that women who are being abused use coping behaviors to survive. [Counselors] can do the abused a disservice if they label these behaviors as "bad" or encourage the women to give them up. What they can do instead is offer her education about the cycle of violence and give her referrals for shelters where she and her children can go for safety. It is the abused woman who knows best what will keep her safe. If this knowledge is not validated and respected, and if she is encouraged to view her ways of coping as negative, her life may be in danger. Labels such as "compulsive caretaking" and "co-dependency"—labels often used to explain the coping behaviors of family and friends of an alcoholic—are not helpful or accurate labels for abused women.

Recovery from domestic violence requires support and a nonjudgmental attitude from individuals who have the courage to reach out and assist the battered woman. Labeling someone who is in crisis does not change the situation for her, nor does it make her escape from abuse any more easily.

Why Women Remain in Battering Relationships

Women remain in abusive relationships for many complex reasons. Fear of retaliation, lack of marketable job skills, and low self-esteem often prevent the battered woman from leaving her abusive partner permanently. Also, as we have already noted, most battered women do not want their marriages to end; they just want the violence to stop. During the "honeymoon" stage of the cycle of abuse, they hold on to the hope that the violence has in fact ended once and for all. It is important to understand their reasons for staying before we can effectively help them:

• *Financial concerns for themselves and for their children hold many women captive to abusive partners.* It is well documented that many single mothers live in poverty. According to *Harvard Business Review*,[4] single parenthood is an increasingly common phenomenon in American society, and about half of the children born in the United States today will spend at least part of their childhood in a single-parent family. Nearly half of these families have incomes below the poverty line. Court-ordered child-support payments represent an inadequate and unreliable source of income for most, and only one out of every three single parents receives child support. Even then, the average yearly payment is only about two thousand dollars. If the battered woman is without adequate job skills, it will be even more difficult for her to manage financially. She may feel that it is easier to literally "take a beating" than to see her children try to survive without proper nutrition, clothing, and decent housing.

• *A major problem for battered women is the inability to access the necessary resources for change.* Resources are available for the battered woman, but she needs a supportive network to refer her to the right places. Many states offer job-training programs to assist individuals who would like further training or who desire to polish their skills and résumés. Some of these programs provide transportation, child-care services, and a small mileage and clothing allowance.

• *Low self-esteem is another major problem among battered women.* A person's self-esteem is based on his or her unique personal experiences and relationships. When a battered woman's self-esteem is so low that she exaggerates self-blame, it is difficult for her to hear Christ's healing words of love and implement his teachings for a healthy and productive life. Many battered women are unable to focus clearly on God's love because they have experienced the wrath of their batterer carried out in God's name. The battered woman may also feel embarrassed by her situation because of our society's often judgmental attitude toward the victims of domestic violence. She feels as though her being beaten is somehow a reflection on her character and worth as a human being. Low self-esteem prevents her not only from leaving the abusive atmosphere but also from seeking help.

• *Battered women often become isolated, cut off from those who could help them.* The isolation techniques that are used by the abuser are intimidating and severe. He controls her every move— where she goes, how much money she spends—and often keeps track of the mileage on her car. These mind games make the battered woman feel as though she is both crazy and incompetent. Most of the time, her days are filled with ideas on how to survive, not how to escape.

• *Fear of accusation and retaliation keeps many women in their abusive relationship.* It is easy to see that many battered women remain in abusive relationships because of fear. They are afraid for their children; they are afraid for their families; they are afraid they cannot make it on their own.

• *Battered women love their husbands, feel sorry for them and their violent behavior, and want to help them.* Many victims of domestic violence view divorce as the abandonment of a person who desperately needs help. They may also believe that they would be breaking their marriage vows, hurting their children, destroying their family, and disobeying God by terminating the relationship. Special sensitivity on the part of pastors should go a long way in assisting the battered woman who feels that God does not wish for her to break the marriage vows. Pastors need to educate themselves about abuse and address problems from the understanding that abuse is an unacceptable behavior.

Battered women are *not* masochistic. During the years that I have counseled battered women, I have never interviewed anyone who enjoyed having her bones broken and her eyes blackened. They don't remain because they like it this way but because they see no way out or they keep hoping things will get better or that it will never happen again.

The Tragedy of Domestic Abuse

It is clear that victimized and abused women are not psychological masochists who enjoy being beaten. Violence does not fill a deep inner need that attracts women to their partners. In many cases, the woman feels responsible for keeping the home together and clings to the hope that the violence will end and that things will get better. Armed with the information in this chapter and a greater understanding of why women remain with or go back to abusive partners, church communities and pastors can come to a greater awareness of the tragedy of domestic abuse. It is of utmost importance and urgency that the faith community not delay in getting involved in this issue that is tearing families apart and causing untold suffering.

NOTES

1. From "For Shelter and Beyond," Massachusetts Coalition of Battered Women's Services and The Women's Coalition, Volunteer Training Manual, Duluth, Minnesota, as reported by NCADV.

2. Joan Zorza, *The Gender Bias Committee's Domestic Violence Study,* 1989, as reported in an NCADV fact sheet.

3. From "Behind the Veil of Silence," pamphlet published by The Hazelden Family Center, Minnesota, as reprinted by Oklahoma Coalition on Domestic Violence and Sexual Assault.

4. Mary Jo Bane and David T. Ellwood, "Is American Business Working for the Poor?" *Harvard Business Review,* September-October 1991, 58.

CHAPTER THREE

Characteristics of the Batterer

Battering is a complex problem; it has no simple solution. Many believe that the only way to prevent violence against women is to change the attitudes and conditions that foster abuse in our society. The church is slowly beginning to acknowledge that violence does actually exist within the "safety" of the faith community. Being able to recognize the characteristics of the abuser will assist the pastor or counselor in assessing the need for intervention.

A man who abuses his partner often exhibits many of the following characteristics and attitudes:

- He blames his victim for his violent behavior: "If you hadn't talked with another man, I would not have lost my temper . . ."
- He denies that he has a problem.
- He frequently denies that he has physically abused his partner, despite bruises and other evidence.
- He seeks to maintain rigid family boundaries (husband, wife, and children against the world).
- He feels impotent and inadequate.
- He has poor communications skills. (Many abusers are capable of good communication on a business or social level but have difficulty communicating on an intimate level.)
- He lacks the ability to trust his partner and cannot appropriately express emotions without violence.
- He is dependent, possessive, and excessively jealous.
- He fears losing the relationship and therefore tries to control his partner.

- He was probably a victim of child abuse.
- He probably witnessed his father abusing his mother.
- He has inadequate parenting skills and creates stress and conflict over parental roles.
- He tends to abuse or neglect his children.
- He views gender roles in rigid stereotypes.
- He has learned negative values regarding the status of women.
- He frequently quotes Scripture regarding gender relationships and preaches the importance of the wife's submission and obedience.

The church community should be alert to a batterer's tendency to harbor rigid expectations of what a wife and family should be. When his wife is unable to live up to his unrealistic goals, he will view this as a serious failure and project anger and blame on her. The batterer has a distorted view of self and others and is unable to identify and accept his own weakness, while at the same time demanding unreasonable perfection from his partner. In one extreme example, an abuser decided that he wanted his wife to look like the airbrushed models on magazine covers. Insisting that his wife lose weight, he forced her, *at gunpoint,* to do two hundred sit-ups every night. By day three, she was so sick that she could hardly walk. She was unable to do the sit-ups, so he gave her two hundred lashings on her bare stomach with a leather belt, all the while telling her that she was lucky not to get two hundred bullets. After he completed his violent punishment, he stormed out of the house. She crawled to the telephone and dialed 911 for help. She was hospitalized for three weeks with internal injuries.

Men that abuse their partners often have a distorted view of God and family. A batterer may feel that God is telling him to abuse his wife and that his family must rely solely upon him for their spiritual identity and direction. But no matter how much a wife may try to live up to a batterer's expectations, her efforts will not be good enough. Many pastors unwisely advise battered women to give the abuser more love and reassurance by being more submissive, but this is not a workable solution because it places the focus of blame and responsibility back on the victim.

It is important for pastors and friends to realize that the abuser's problem is rooted in his long-term feelings about himself. Most controllers and batterers actually feel very powerless inside. Good self-esteem and a sense of inner control are generally lacking in the abuser, so he blames his partner and actually sees himself as the victim. He feels that he must control his entire family and that he is entitled to do so. So when his partner does something that he disagrees with, he feels justified in threatening and abusing her.

After he has cooled off, the abuser may feel humiliated and ashamed. He will probably know that something is wrong with his behavior but won't be able to figure it all out without help. Batterers *can* learn how to change their destructive course if their motivation to change is sincere—but to change will take a lot of hard work, honesty, and outside support.

Assessment Tools

The "violence wheel" and the "nonviolence wheel" [1] are graphics that contain characteristics typical of violent and nonviolent behavior. The violence wheel is often used by professionals who treat batterers and is also used in domestic violence programs, particularly with support groups. It is a concise profile of a batterer. Women can begin to see the level of violence they are experiencing by noting how many of the characteristics are exhibited by their abuser. At the center of the violence wheel are the words "power and control" because these are what dominate the abuser's behavior. In general, he is inappropriately jealous of his partner's friends, family, and coworkers and will keep her isolated from them, in addition to the other abusive actions.

The nonviolence wheel, on the other hand, reflects the functional family system. "Equality" is the central motivator of the nonabusive male, and he will rely on shared tasks and responsible parenting rather the tactics of the one who desires control because he is the "master of the castle." The nonbattering male can be trusted to be honest and accountable for his actions. In turn, he will trust and respect his partner and support her own personal goals and will show in other ways a mutual partnership.

Violence Wheel

Using Privilege: Treating her like a servant; making all the big decisions; acting like the "master of the castle"; being the one to define roles

Using Children: Making her feel guilty about the children; using the children to relay messages; using visitation to harass her; threatening to take the children away

Minimizing, Denying & Blaming: Making light of the abuse and not taking her concerns about it seriously; saying the abuse didn't happen; shifting responsibility for abusive behavior; saying she caused it

Using Isolation: Controlling what she does, who she sees and talks to, what she reads, where she goes; limiting her outside involvement; using jealousy to justify actions

Using Emotional Abuse: Putting her down; making her feel bad about herself; calling her names; making her think she's crazy; playing mind games; humiliating her; making her feel guilty

Using Intimidation: Making her afraid by using looks, actions, gestures; smashing things; destroying her property; abusing pets; displaying weapons

Using Coercion & Threats: Making and/or carrying out threats to do something to hurt her; threatening to leave her; threatening to commit suicide; threatening to report her to welfare; making her drop charges; making her do illegal things

Using Economic Abuse: Preventing her from getting or keeping a job; making her ask for money; taking her money; not letting her know about or have access to family income

Nonviolence Wheel

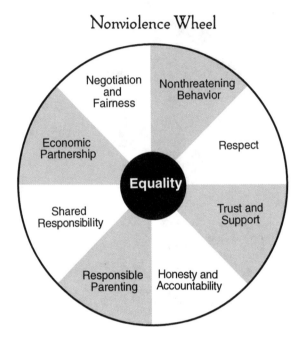

Shared Responsibility: Mutually agreeing on a fair distribution of work; making family decisions together

Responsible Parenting: Sharing parental responsibilities together; being a positive non-violent role model for the children

Honesty & Accountability: Accepting responsibility for self; acknowledging responsibility for past use of violence; admitting being wrong; communicating openly and truthfully

Trust and Support: Supporting her goals in life; respecting her right to her own feelings, friends, activities, and opinions

Respect: Listening to her non-judgmentally; being emotionally affirming and understanding; valuing opinions

Nonthreatening Behavior: Talking and acting so that she feels safe and comfortable expressing herself and doing things

Negotiation and Fairness: Seeking mutually satisfying resolutions to conflicts; accepting change; being willing to compromise

Economic Partnership: Making money decisions together; making sure both partners benefit from financial arrangements

The Historic Acceptance of Violence against Women

Violence against women is as old as recorded history, and throughout the ages it has been upheld by both civil and religious authorities. Our language's history reveals some interesting earlier attitudes toward wife abuse. For instance, the origin of the common phrase "rule of thumb" lies in English common law from centuries past. Under that law, called the "Rule of Thumb," a man was allowed to whip his wife with a stick, as long as it was no bigger than his thumb. Prior to the Rule of Thumb, a man could use anything he wanted to beat his wife; so the advent of this rule was a major reform for women!

What Is Domestic Violence under the Law?

The legal definition of domestic violence includes beating; using weapons such as a knife; gun; or hammer; slapping; pushing; throwing down; throwing an object at or near the victim; or verbal threats ("If you leave me, I will kill you.)

Battering is considered a misdemeanor in most states rather than a felony, yet injuries suffered by battered women are at least as serious as injuries suffered in 90 percent of violent felony crimes.[2] We as a society must ask why this discrepancy exists and why the court system doesn't do more to protect battered women. We must also demand laws that protect women and punish the men who abuse them, thus asserting that wife battering is indeed a serious crime.

Stalking, one part of the whole picture of abuse, is being addressed by laws in many states. California passed the first anti-stalking law in 1990, and by 1992 twenty-eight more states had passed such laws. It is likely that even more states have anti-stalking laws on the books as of this writing. Make sure to find out what your state laws are. Laws can be of great value, but there must be significant evidence in order for a ruling to be made in the woman's favor. In North Carolina, for example, the battered woman must keep a careful log of the dates and times that she was stalked. If she and her abuser have been living separately for a significant time period, this strengthens her case considerably because it proves to the court that she is serious about ending the relationship.

When You Call the Police

Be serious! In many cases if you make multiple calls to the police within a forty-eight-hour period, and if they reasonably believe that you do not need help, then they do not have to respond to your calls. For example, if you call the police and tell them that you need their help and then call them back and tell them you have changed your mind, they might give your case less consideration.

When the police arrive, be sure to give them any pictures, torn or bloody clothing, and any other evidence of the attack. If the abuser has violated a court order, give the police a copy of it so they can make an arrest. Also, if you have divorce or legal-separation papers, show these to the responding officer.

The Role of the Faith Community

Even now, in most faith communities, wife beating has been largely ignored as a social concern and is still brushed aside as a private, family matter. But ignoring the issue does not make it go away. Every fifteen seconds a woman is battered in this country. Thus it is more critical than ever for the faith community to boldly step forward and courageously clear away the debris of neglect, ignorance, and misunderstanding surrounding the issue of domestic violence. Each of us was created from God's love so that we might carry the message of love to those who are in need of healing and wholeness. Members of the faith community must bring God's grace to those suffering or inflicting abuse; they must not be afraid to get involved and work to alleviate situations of abuse. Armed with knowledge that helps identify problems and with information about local agencies and resources, church pastors and members can be a lifeline to women who are suffering abuse.

Help for the Abuser

To help end an abusive relationship, we can either offer the abused woman the spiritual, emotional, and financial help she needs to start a new life—or we can try to help her abuser change. Over the past ten years, the number of batterers' treatment programs has risen across the United States, but the success rate for changing the abuser's violent behavior is, unfortunately, still very low.

"One problem is that men grow up in a society that tells them it is acceptable to resolve their problems through violence," explains one man who works as a counselor in a well-known batterers' treatment program. "Most of them would come into the treatment center with a 'Rambo' attitude. During my five years of running groups for batterers, I did not hear one abuser accept full responsibility for his violence. Their constant excuse was that 'she wouldn't shut up' or 'she wouldn't do what I told her to do.'

"Breaking through the barrier of the abuser's rationalization and denial is the biggest job for any counselor working with batterers," he says. "These men must first come to terms with themselves, admitting that they have a problem, before treatment works. For the majority of the men in my groups, attendance had been mandated by a judge. It was obvious that, for the most part, they were there because they didn't want to go to jail. I frequently challenged them when they started playing tough guy, telling them that while I may hold a black belt in karate, I never felt the need to beat my wife or control my family. This almost always made them take notice. Some of them would hang around after the group ended, asking me questions about how I managed my anger. Those were the guys that truly desired change, but unfortunately, they were few and far between."

Many believe that alcohol or drug abuse is a primary cause for violent behavior. But according to authors Howard Holtz and Kathleen Furness,[4] more than one-third of violent partners do not drink. Further, if alcohol and drugs are involved in the relationship, frequently the violence continues even after treatment. Most researchers and counselors have found that while substance abuse is a *symptom* in some batterers, it is not the *cause* of physical violence.[5] According to Evan Stark and Ann Flitcraft, alcohol is a factor in fewer than 8 percent of the domestic violence cases where police are called.[6] While alcohol probably increases the *risk* of abusive violence, in lieu of conclusive evidence, it should be considered a contextual factor, to be treated separately from violence.

All studies indicate that battering is learned behavior. Between 60 and 80 percent of batterers grew up watching their fathers abuse their mothers. Most professional counselors who work specifically with batterers, along with social scientists and researchers, agree that men who were beaten as children or observed their mothers being beaten are more likely to exhibit violent behavior, as violence becomes an acceptable expression of emotion. Often, an abuser will tell his partner that God has miraculously transformed him, and he will promise to never assault her again. He will tell her that he has changed, and perhaps, within that emotional moment of begging her to return, he actually means what he says. Yet in the majority of cases, he will revert to battering her within a short time after she returns to him. Clearly, men who batter their wives are acting in direct opposition to their marriage vows.

Because domestic violence is directly related to social and cultural practices, I believe that a batterer who truly desires change can eventually, through hard work and determination, *unlearn* his violent behavior patterns and experience inner healing. Batterers need to be told by other men that violent behavior is unacceptable. They also need to know that Jesus loved them so much that he died for them—and that, in order for a man to be in line with God's spiritual laws, he should love his wife in the same manner. Batterers desperately need professional help, prayer, and the love and peace of God.

NOTES

1. Adapted from the Domestic Abuse Intervention Project's (Duluth, Minnesota) use of "Domestic Violence: The Facts," Battered Women Fighting Back!, Inc., Boston, Massachusetts.

2. Joan Zorza, *The Gender Bias Committee's Domestic Violence Study*, 1989, as reported in an NCADV fact sheet.

3. American Medical Association, 1991.

4. Howard Holtz and Kathleen Furness, "The Health Care Provider's Role in Domestic Violence," *Trends in Health Care, Law & Ethics*, vol. 8, no. 2, Spring 1993, 48.

5. Richard Oppel, Jr., "Seizing Control Through Pain," *Fort Worth Star Telegram*, April 5, 1992.

6. Evan Stark and Ann Flitcraft, "Violence Among Intimates: An Epidemiological Review," *Handbook of Family Violence*, Von Haselt ed., et. al. (New York: Plenum Press, 1988), 309.

CHAPTER FOUR

The Cycle of Abuse

Domestic violence professionals who have studied family violence and the battering of women describe three stages of abuse. It is crucial that pastors and church members be aware not only of the characteristics of the battered woman and her batterer, but also of the stages of abuse. In recognizing the pattern, one can begin to predict when violence may erupt or be most likely to happen; steps can then be taken for an abused woman to remove herself from immediate danger. Being able to identify stage two, for example, could possibly save a woman's life, for it is during this time that the possibility exists for the victim to be murdered. Your role as helper is to emphasize that the violence is not the fault of the victim. It would be helpful to have available the number of an appropriate hotline and write it down for her. Be careful not to identify the number with the words "battered" or "violence," which would place her in more danger if her partner found it.

These are the three cyclical stages of abuse:

• *Stage one.* A period of growing tension. During this phase, the abuser becomes irritated by matters that he would have considered trivial during the so-called honeymoon stage (stage 3). He is argumentative and verbally abusive.

• *Stage two.* An explosion of anger and violence, lasting from a few hours to a few days or up to several weeks. During phase two, women are seriously injured, even murdered by their abusers. The second stage of violence is the most dangerous, and women should be encouraged to seek temporary refuge during this time period.

• *Stage three.* A cooling-off or "honeymoon" period when the relationship improves. During this phase, the woman who has left her partner generally returns because he promises to change his violent behavior and becomes more attentive and romantic, often showering her with gifts and declarations of devotion.

Identifying Stages of Abuse

Stage one of the cycle of abuse can begin by the batterer nagging his partner about the way she has prepared dinner. She may notice that when he arrives home from work, he throws his briefcase across the room and yells at the dog and kids. When sitting down at the dinner table, he may start complaining about the roast being too dry or the vegetables being overcooked. She tries to pacify him by remaining cheerful. She apologizes for the meal. She apologizes for *his* bad day at work. He tells her that she can't do anything right and then slams out of the house. This behavior might continue for several days, during which time everyone in the household tiptoes around and tries to stay out of the abuser's path; then behavior signaling the start of stage two begins.

Stage two of the abuse might begin by the abuser coming home from work and becoming confrontational with his partner. He may ask irrational questions, and the conversation might go something like this:

Abuser: "Why did you look at me like that?"

Partner: "Like what?"

Abuser: "Don't try and lie your way out of it! You just gave me a dirty look and you know it!"

At this point in the cycle, it will not matter very much how she answers him. If she denies the accusation, he will call her a liar, and this will result in a beating. If she admits that she gave him a dirty look just to satisfy her abuser, he will still become violent. It is during phase two that many women are seriously injured or even killed. This phase can last for several hours, days, or even weeks. Many women are brutally beaten, terrorized, tortured, and held captive by their abusers during this stage of the abuse cycle.

Stage three of the cycle is commonly referred to as the honeymoon period. This stage usually occurs after the battered woman escapes or presses charges against her partner. The abuser has had time to cool off and realizes that his partner may not come back. He tells her that he will change but that she must be there to help him make a new start. He usually promises to seek counseling if she will return. He is more attentive and loving, and may send flowers and cards. Unfortunately, this cycle usually lasts long enough to get her back into the home. Then after a few days, or if she is lucky, a few weeks, the cycle of abuse begins again with stage one.

How Do We Help Stop the Violence?

- Hold batterers accountable for their actions and do not allow them to hold leadership positions in the church.
- Provide intervention for battered women by offering them nonjudgmental counsel and resources for safety.
- Develop effective batterer treatment programs in your church and community.
- Organize a committee of interested persons to brainstorm ways to get the church involved in stopping the cycle of abuse. Include an equal number of men and women and invite domestic violence professionals from shelters and batterer treatment centers.

Stories of Abuse

In order to help a woman who is being battered, we must learn not to judge them too harshly or come up with quick-fix solutions or suggestions for their spouses or their situations. The following women's stories are a few of those I have heard over the years. As you will see, these women often survived by their own wit and determination, despite a lack of help from their pastors and churches, who were obviously uninformed about domestic abuse. Listening carefully and openly to battered women's often-dramatic stories can help us understand their experiences, identify some of the characteristics they exhibit and which stage of the abuse they are in, and give them hope for a better life. As we listen to their stories and offer our hand of friendship, we assure them that they are not alone.

As you read the following stories, see if you can identify some characteristics of battered women and their batterers, as well as the stages of abuse. You might also want to reread Kimberly's story (chapter 1) with this information in mind. (In chapter 6, we will learn how to "actively listen" to battered women—and to respond in more appropriate and responsible ways than the pastors and churches from whom these women sought help.)

Angela

Angela's husband began abusing her shortly after their honeymoon. "It didn't seem like 'wife abuse' at the time," she said. "I just thought that he was a little more possessive than average. At first he did not leave any bruises on me, so I didn't think that I was officially being abused.

"He was the associate pastor of a mainline denomination. My job was to make him look good. If he thought I was spending too much time with my family, he would reprimand me in front of the entire congregation. He conducted a lot of the nighttime services, and that's when he would preach on submission and say that wives should obey their husbands, no matter what. He would even go so far as to tell the men in his fellowship that women should be disciplined when necessary, especially if such action might prevent their wives from going to hell. Anytime I was late getting his dinner, or if I ever dared to disagree with him, he would let me know right away that my mind belonged to him and that it was his duty and responsibility to correct my errors. I was constantly walking on eggshells; I never knew when his anger would erupt into violence."

Angela's turning point came when she decided to take a full-time position as an executive secretary for a Fortune 500 company. Due to a decline in church membership, her husband had been forced to take a cut in his salary. "It was the opportunity of a lifetime," she smiled. "Dan knew that I'd be working a lot of overtime. He didn't seem to mind, largely because we were so far behind on our bills, and the extra money I made would help to get us back on our feet.

"One day when I had to put in a thirteen-hour day, I called to let him know I'd be late. He hit the roof, demanding that I quit my job on the spot and come home. When I refused, he promised me a beating for disobeying him. That night, when I walked into the house, tired from my long day, he was waiting for me with a Bible in one hand and a belt in the other. He read Scriptures on submission that I'd never even heard of! In retrospect, I think that he made most of it up as he went along. He accused me of having an affair with my new boss, and then, before I knew it, he was pushing me against the wall, hitting my face with the belt buckle and twisting my arm. As he hit me again and again and quoted Scriptures, I screamed out at him in defense for the first time, telling him he was nothing more than a wolf in sheep's clothing. Of course, this only made matters worse, and he ended up breaking my jaw. I was out of work for two weeks. As soon as I was well enough, I packed my bags while Dan was at church and moved to another town."

Catherine

"He kept his Bible covered in a leather zipper case and would sort of prop it on his shoulder, walking back and forth, quoting Scripture that I'd never heard before," said Catherine, her eyes swelling with tears as she recalled the abusive situation. "If I was ten minutes late getting home from the grocery store, he'd accuse me of running around on him. Once, I caught him tearing pages out of my Bible—pages of Scripture that had been of comfort to me that I had underlined. My favorite was Psalm 91. He told me that he would tell me what I could and could not read. He had to be in total control of my life. He sometimes even followed me into the bathroom while I bathed.

"Just before I left him for good, he held me down on the sofa and called me a freak of nature. I'd had to have a hysterectomy three months earlier, and he considered this an attack against his manhood because I would not be able to have more children. He then ordered our fourteen-year-old son to go to the gun cabinet and load the .300 magnum so that he could kill me. But instead of going to get the gun, my son ran out to the neighbor's house and called the police. By the time law enforcement arrived twenty minutes later, they found me on my knees with my hands tied behind my back, begging my husband not to kill me. They talked him down, and finally he handed over the gun that he had been pointing at the back of my head.

"They told me I could press charges. I did so, knowing that he would finish the job as soon as someone posted his bail. My son begged me to pack up our station wagon and leave town. He knew that his father would probably come after us both for calling in the police. So we left the state in the middle of the night. We packed our car with everything imaginable, knowing that there was no turning back. I had fifty dollars that I'd been saving for the previous three months, stashing away a dollar here and a dollar there, in hopes of accumulating enough money to eventually escape. I took it from its hiding place and called my cousin, who lived over a thousand miles away, from a pay phone. I didn't want to call her from my home phone because I didn't want her number to show up on the next month's bill. She wanted to wire me the money so that our trip to her place would be easier, but I knew there was no time for that.

"We slept in rest areas and lived on peanut butter, crackers, Kool-Aid, and canned tins of meat that I had hurriedly confiscated from my kitchen cabinets. I made my son a bed in the back seat. We kept our doors locked at all times, and I slept with one eye open throughout the week-long journey. I wasn't afraid of the monsters in the rest areas," Catherine laughed. "I was afraid that somehow my husband would get out of jail and find us before I could get to my cousin's place. When we finally arrived, I slept for two days and then went out looking for a job. I managed to get employment at a major department store and worked my way into a management position within one year.

"But it took me five years to get up the courage to file for a divorce. I didn't want the hassle of communicating with my husband, and I wanted to wait until our son reached legal age so that he would not be drawn into a dangerous custody battle. My son was terrified of his father, and with good reason. He would have run away rather that agreeing to visit his dad.

"In retrospect, I realize that my husband was very much out of order spiritually for all that he did to me. The church that we attended enabled his violence toward me; the pastor never reprimanded him for his abuse. In fact, I knew of several other wives in the church who were being abused by their husbands and went to the pastor for help. They were made to feel as though it was something they had asked for!"

Most of the time it takes a near-death situation for the battered woman to leave her partner. In Catherine's case, the horror of her husband commanding their son to load the weapon precipitated her departure.

Linda

"People would come up to me at church and tell me what a fine Christian man Jack was. Then we'd go home from church and something would set him off. Usually he would be mad at the preacher for giving other men in the congregation more attention than he felt they deserved. Jack always felt that his good works outweighed those of other church leaders. But he would never allow anyone in the congregation to see his abusive side.

"Once, when I'd had enough of Jack's abuse, I went to our preacher and asked him to talk to Jack. I entered his office with a black eye and my right foot in a cast because Jack had pushed me off the front porch for 'not tending to our flowers properly.' The preacher listened to my story and just laughed, saying that he would never have dreamed that Jack had a temper. Then he proceeded to ask me what I had done to cause the abuse. Was I being a caring and sensitive wife? Were we having sex often enough to fulfill my marital obligations? I couldn't believe my ears! I would not have gone back to church at all after that, but Jack made me go."

Lauren

"It was like living with two different people," said Lauren. "Sometimes Billy could be so thoughtful and sweet that I'd be in awe. He'd go to church, stand up and testify about all the wonderful things that God had done in his life. He would take his place in the prayer line with the other elders of the congregation and lay hands on members of the church who were sick. The pastor actually seemed to think that the sun rose and set on Billy's spiritual strength!

"Once, after Billy had dislocated my jaw, I got up the nerve to go and talk to our pastor about the abuse that had been taking place for the entire ten years of our marriage."

"And was your pastor helpful?" I asked.

Lauren laughed cynically. "Helpful to Billy. The pastor called Billy at his workplace and told him that I had been in his office and was very unhappy. Billy came home and beat me again and then locked me in a dark closet. I was there for two days, without food or water or bathroom facilities. He told me that he was disciplining me for not submitting properly. Finally he allowed me to come out after I promised that I would never discuss our 'personal family matters' with anyone again."

"Did you continue to attend church with Billy?"

"Yes. He wouldn't have had it any other way. And everyone looked at me as though I were some kind of criminal because he told them that I had inflicted injuries upon myself and had falsely accused him."

"That's incredible," I remarked, angry yet at the same time amazed at Billy's ability to charm the other church members.

"Of course it's incredible," she said, "but you have to remember that Billy presented an entirely different side to his fellow church members. I mean, here was a man who helped little old ladies into their pews on Sunday morning and contributed 10 percent of his income to the church. It didn't matter that I attended church with bruises on my neck and arms, or that sometimes I was so battered that I couldn't go out of the house for weeks."

"Did anyone from your church ever call and check on you when you didn't attend services?" I asked.

"No. Billy had them believing that I was out with the flu or that our five-year-old daughter was sick and I needed to stay home. He could manipulate coworkers and church members into believing anything he said.

"I was no different in some respects," she said, slightly lowering her head. "On more than one occasion he had me believing that he would never hurt me again. There would be tender moments when

I was convinced that everything would be all right and that the abuse was over. Then the nightmare would start up again."

"How did you manage to escape?"

"I left him while he was teaching a Sunday school class," she replied. "On this particular morning, I convinced him that we should drive separate automobiles so that I wouldn't have to attend the adult Bible class. I told him that I felt really bad that morning and wanted to sleep in for a little longer, but that I would see him at the eleven o'clock service. I knew that Billy would never leave the church to come looking for me, and as soon as he was out the door, I jumped out of bed and began packing suitcases for my daughter and me.

"My aunt had visited us a few weeks earlier, suspected that something was wrong, and taken me aside to talk. When she left, she gave me the number of the shelter in a neighboring town. I asked if she would check it out and call me on the following day. She did so, and, for the first time in many years, I felt there might be hope for my daughter and me. When I talked to the shelter staff, they told me that if I wasn't in immediate danger, I should carefully plan my escape. So each day for the next several weeks, I got organized, stashing away the things that I wanted and throwing out the items that I didn't want to take along. I gathered important papers and made little coded lists. By the time I should have been walking into the eleven o'clock service, my daughter and I were on the road to safety. We remained in that particular shelter for thirty days and then were transferred to another state, where I found a job waitressing. It worked out really well in the long run because my younger sister wanted to relocate with us, and she baby-sat my daughter while I attended night classes."

"What about child custody and other legal matters?" I asked.

"I took a chance and never contacted Billy about any of it. I knew that if he had our daughter and I was not there to protect her, he would probably hurt her. He had spanked her with a belt just before my aunt informed me of the shelter, and I was becoming fearful of his violence toward her. My daughter had nightmares about going back to her father without me; she had been a witness to the violence since birth. Somehow it didn't seem right to send her back into the home, which is exactly what would have happened had I pursued legal custody and divorce. I was able to make a choice and escaped the violent household. I felt that I owed her the same. I decided that if she wanted to seek out her father when she was an adult, then that would be her choice, and I would not interfere. I was even prepared for her to hold me responsible for not having a relationship with her father. But as a young adult she thanks me for getting us out of the violence, and, as far as I know, she has no desire to contact her father."

Conclusion

Lauren's fear for her child's safety is not uncommon among women who have escaped violence. Many victims of domestic violence disappear with their children in order to protect them from abuse. The woman who chooses this path in order to protect her children faces a tremendous challenge, for she cannot risk applying for any government assistance without supplying "good cause" for her husband not to be contacted for child support. It would logically seem that leaving the trauma of domestic violence would be sufficient, but this is not always the case. I have discovered that many battered women do not want to risk being found by their abusers, so they frequently choose anonymity over abuse by taking jobs that pay "under the table" until their children reach adulthood.

CHAPTER FIVE

When Children Are Involved

When children are a part of the family, women often find it more difficult to leave a violent partner. The challenge of single parenting, especially when the woman has no place to go, no job skills, and no money, often makes her feel forced to "wait it out" until the children are grown.

But by that time it is often too late—for the futures of both her and the children. She has probably become severely crippled physically, emotionally, and/or spiritually; she may even be killed while "waiting it out." And the children have become deeply entrenched in the violence. Physically, emotionally, and spiritually injured, they are poised to carry the fury on to the next generation by either marrying an abuser or becoming the perpetrator in this narrative of destruction. Furthermore, they are likely to become targets or victims of their father's violence. It has been shown that 70 percent of men who abuse their female partners also abuse their children.[1] Another study has indicated that, as violence against women becomes more severe and frequent in the home, children experience a 300 percent increase in physical violence by the male batterer.[2] The symptoms are cyclical, for up to 70 percent of men who abuse their wives or partners grew up witnessing their fathers abuse their mothers. Children who live in violent homes come to accept brutality as a way of life—and pass it on.

Children who come out of violent homes carry with them a painful burden. They are hurt and frightened to see their mothers pushed around, and even if they are not themselves physically abused, they frequently display the same characteristics as children who have been abused. Of children who witness their mothers being abused by their fathers, 40 percent suffer from anxiety, 48 percent suffer from depression, 53 percent act out with their parents, and 60 percent act out with their siblings.[3] These children also suffer poor health, low self-esteem, poor impulse control, sleeping difficulties, and feelings of powerlessness. They are at high risk for alcohol and drug use, sexual abuse and promiscuity, running away from home, isolation, loneliness, fear, and suicide.[4] In addition, according to the U.S. Census Bureau (1991), children comprise 50 percent of the poor in America, making them more likely to become poor than any other age group.

Abusive partners often use children as pawns in custody fights to coerce their female partners to reconcile with them. These coercive incidents frequently occur during court-ordered visitation.[5]

Jane

The fears women have about "making it on their own" rather than "waiting it out" are realistic. Jane took her two children, ages twelve and thirteen, and left her abusive husband, only to end up living in a housing project beset by drugs, street violence, and gangs. Survivors of domestic abuse sometimes feel that they have traded one prison for another. Jane feared for her children's lives and safety during this time; she made them stay at home and play in their small apartment except when they had to go to school.

"It was a nightmare," said Jane. "When I left my abusive husband, I had to give up my home in the suburbs and move into the housing project. I didn't have a choice. The house was in my name as well as his, but I couldn't afford an attorney. My husband would not file for divorce because he knew that if he did, I would have access to the court system and the judge, with or without an attorney. And even if the judge had awarded me our house, I would not have been able to keep up the mortgage payments of over seven hundred dollars a month."

"What about child-support payments?" I inquired.

"The welfare department turned my case over to the child-support enforcement agency, and the state took my husband to court for nonpayment. The child-support enforcement office would take him to court for nonpayment, and the judge would order him to pay the past due amount. He would always come up with a sob story, and the child-support agency would allow him to make up his past due amount in monthly payments. Then, after about three months, he'd stop paying again, and the process began from square one—which would take months.

"I applied for A.F.D.C. [Aid for Families of Dependent Children] and was awarded $186 per month for two children. I also received food stamps, which helped a great deal, and Medicaid, a real blessing from God, as it allowed my children and me to receive free medical care. I found a part-time job waiting tables and made about eighty dollars a week. But in doing so, I lost my Medicaid and part of the food stamps I was receiving. So I decided to quit work and go back to school and get a degree. I arranged my classes so that I would be home when the children came in from school because I knew that I would have to supervise them closely. There were drug dealers outside our door almost all of the time. The police would come around every now and then and do a drug bust. Things would settle down for about a week. Then, like vermin, they'd be back, trafficking cocaine, crack, anything a person wanted. At night, my kids would turn off the lights and watch the drug dealers come out. Some of the tenants would participate in buying and selling, but many of them were law-abiding citizens like me who couldn't afford to live anywhere else.

"It was tempting, on many occasions, to return to my home in the suburbs and be a housewife. My husband constantly begged me to come home. He was an engineer and made a terrific salary. He was a good husband and provider when he wasn't beating me and scaring the children. I came very close to going back, but I stuck to my goal of getting a degree, and God protected my children and me."

Jane is now a registered nurse and makes over forty thousand dollars a year. But it was not an easy journey for her and her children. If she had been able to hire an attorney, she would have at least had some money from the divorce settlement that would have made her life less difficult. Statistics reveal that in the first year after separation or divorce, a woman's standard of living drops by 73 percent, while a man's improves by an average of 42 percent.[6] This, of course, also has significant effects on the children and their well-being.

Linda

Linda's situation posed some different personal and legal problems when she tried, unsuccessfully, to find a way out for herself and her five children—her "babies" (ages one to five).

"I've tried to leave him more times than I can remember, but I always end up going back home. The last time I left, I went through the court system for a restraining order. The judge gave me temporary custody of our five children but granted Tommy visitation rights every other weekend, even though he had left a hand mark on our four-year-old's face. Social Services investigated the incident because I reported my husband's abuse to them. But when the social worker came out to the house and talked to us, she decided to charge both my husband *and me* with neglect."

"Why on earth were you charged with neglect?" I asked.

"Because the social worker said that domestic violence was bad for the children and that I had contributed to the abuse by staying in the home. She didn't take into consideration the fact that I had called the police when my husband hit our four-year-old. She just decided that my husband was abusive—and that I was neglectful for staying."

"Was the judge aware of all this when he gave your husband regular visitation rights?" I inquired.

"Oh yes, he knew all about it. But he said that there were four other children to consider besides our four-year-old. No reports of abuse had been filed against my husband regarding the other children, and, since a social worker was visiting the home on a regular weekly schedule and there had been no further incidents of abuse, he would not deny my husband his fatherly rights."

"So how did that work out?" I asked curiously.

"It was a nightmare," Linda replied, her eyes welling up with tears. "Every time he came to Mama's house—that's where the babies and I were staying—he ranted and raved at me, insisting that I come back home. This caused the babies to start crying, and it just tore me all to pieces. On more than one occasion, he became physically abusive with me, slamming me up against the wall and threatening my life. But when Mama called the police, they wouldn't do anything."

"Do you mean the police would not arrest him?"

"Right. They just told him to go somewhere and cool off. And of course, he had the babies with him, and I never knew what he would do to them after a violent encounter with me. I worried myself sick every time he had them because I was not there to protect them."

"I'm sure it must have been terribly frightening for you," I consoled.

"It's hard to leave when there are five children to care for. Every time I try to get away from him, I get pulled back in. I worry about him hurting my kids when I'm not there to protect them. And it's impossible for me to hold down a job for any length of time because one of them almost always has the sniffles, and it takes every penny that I earn to pay for the children's day care."

"What about your family?" I asked. "Would they be willing to help out until you could get on your feet?"

"My mother allowed me to live with her for a while, but she got pretty tired of my husband coming around and threatening her. I would love to go back to school and get a degree in nursing, but he'd never allow that. I guess I'll just have to wait it out until the kids are older."

Libby

To look at Libby, one might never suspect that she had ever been a battered woman. She was happy and relaxed, a successful real estate broker with her own business and full-time staff. As Libby tells the amazing story of her escape from her abusive husband five years ago, it is clear that her three children were affected by the

violence despite her attempts to protect them. She began by recall-
ing her concern for them.

"I tried on numerous occasions to hide the abuse from the
children, but in retrospect, I realize that they knew exactly what was
going on. They heard their daddy beating me, then saw my bruises
on the following day and would ask what had happened. I'd lie,
telling them that I had fallen or bumped against something.

"On this particular night, my husband was so loud and violent
that all three of my children got out of bed and were crying and
screaming during the entire episode. He quoted Bible verses such
as 'Ask and ye shall receive.' He insisted that I'd asked for the
violence and accused me of being unfaithful—which I wasn't. He
said I'd receive what I had asked for! Isn't that just about the nuttiest
Scripture interpretation you have ever heard?

"When he heard all three of our little girls screaming, he momen-
tarily snapped out of it and slammed out of the house. But I knew
that he would drive around town for a few minutes and work himself
up into an even angrier state. So while he was gone, my five-year-
old daughter helped dress her three- and four-year-old sisters while
I threw clothes, toothbrushes, and all sorts of strange things into a
suitcase. When you're in the middle of a crisis, you don't know how
to think, much less pack. [See Appendix B for guidance on how
women can prepare for such an emergency exit.] I remember
opening up the suitcase twenty-four hours later and wondering how
I had known what to pack—and why I had included my winter coat
and snow boots for all of the girls—in July!

"Just as I was buckling my three-year-old into her car seat, I saw
my husband's headlights and knew I'd better get out of there fast.
I quickly put the van in reverse; I knew he would have tried to block
me in the driveway. If that had happened, I might never have gotten
out alive. He made several attempts to run me off the road, but I
managed to hold my own while I headed straight for the police
station, with all my girls screaming and crying."

"And did you request a warrant?" I asked.

"No, because just as I pulled into the police station, he slowed
down and did not follow me into the parking lot. I was afraid of
pressing charges because he had always threatened to kill me if I

did so. But at the same time, I wanted him to think that I might take the chance, mainly because he was so frightened by the prospect of being ruined in the community by the publicity involved in criminal charges. He was a well-known member of the community and church. His ego couldn't have handled negative media attention."

"What did you do? Where did you go?" I asked.

"Well, that's when my second major set of problems began," she said. "The local shelter for battered women was full. They advised me to go to the next county—but I didn't have enough gas in my car to get to the next county! I went to the homeless shelter about five miles away, but they wouldn't admit me into their program because I was a battered woman. Their policy was due to the fact that battered women brought with them an entirely different set of problems than a typical homeless person: there was always an abuser in the background who might threaten everyone in sight—which of course placed the other residents' lives in danger."

Libby looked out the window for a moment. "It's such a beautiful day," she said. "Everything looks brighter and clearer now that I am out of the violence. I really don't think that I'll ever take anything for granted again—not after some of the dark nights of my past."

"What did you do, Libby, after the homeless shelter turned you away?" I asked.

Tears filled Libby's eyes. "I literally begged them to let us stay, but they wouldn't do it. Finally I just started going around to different motels, asking them if they would give my kids and me a place to stay for the night. At last, one man took pity on us and gave us a room. The following morning I called my mother and asked her if the kids and I could stay with her. She reluctantly agreed, for she was living in a small, two-bedroom apartment, and my kids, as young as they were, got on her nerves. A few days passed, and my husband found me and kept calling me, begging me to come home. I had no money, no job, no day care. I went back home because I felt I had no other choice."

Unfortunately, Libby's story is not uncommon. There is not enough long-term support available to women, especially those with children who try to leave an abusive partner. Due to space limitations, for every one woman accepted into a battered women's shelter, two women and her children are turned away. In some urban areas, five to seven women are turned away for every two women served.

A woman who has children and is seeking shelter also has a far more difficult time financially. Finding low-income housing frequently entails a twelve- to eighteen-month waiting period, and welfare checks can take up to three months to process. This is why a coordinated community response from all service providers *and churches* is essential—to ensure effective intervention to protect victims and stop the violence by batterers.

Four years after that desperate night, Libby made the final break. "I was washing dishes one evening after supper, and he came in from work in a terribly foul mood—worse than I had ever seen. Our eldest daughter, who was nine by that time, was talking on the telephone to one of her friends. My husband jerked the phone out of the wall and sent her to her room. Our other two girls were upstairs doing homework, and I breathed a sigh of relief that they would not witness their father's violence. (They later told me that they always knew when he was beating me, and I realized that I had really fooled myself into believing that I could protect them.)

"This time he accused me of flirting with our neighbor across the street. He had seen me talking to him the previous day and had decided that I was having an affair. I cringed as he began to quote Scriptures because I knew the beatings were always worse when he recited Bible verses. I think he felt absolved when he used the Bible. The beating must have gone on for over an hour, and in the process he punctured my eardrum and broke my wrist, not to mention all of the welts and bruises that covered my body. At some point I passed out; when I came to, I was in an ambulance. My eldest daughter had called 911, which had brought not only the police but also an ambulance and a social worker."

"And what did the social worker do?" I inquired, half expecting to hear that Libby had been charged with neglect.

"She was wonderful," Libby said. "She noted the nature of the violence and recommended that the children be placed in foster care until I was released from the hospital. After a week or so, she brought me a list of shelter programs throughout the state and suggested that I make every effort to terminate my relationship with my husband. My husband was charged with neglect, and a judge granted me assistance in going back home to retrieve my belongings. I feared that if I remained with him any longer, he would either kill me or I would end up losing custody of my children—or both. I went into a shelter for a couple of weeks and then made arrangements to go live with my aunt in another state.

"While staying with her, I was able to go back to school and get my life back. The children had to go see their father twice a year for visitation. I had a terribly difficult time with that, but somehow, by the grace of God, I was able to let them go without feeling as though I had to be there to protect them. I knew that they were all capable of dialing 911 if necessary, and I instructed them to do so if their daddy became abusive. After a couple of extended visits, which he had valiantly fought for, he became disinterested in the children and focused his attention on a new girlfriend, who eventually became his wife. They now have two children, and my girls never hear from him, not even at Christmas. But in the long run it is probably in their best interest because at least they have been permanently sealed out of the violence."

Legal Issues

Why was Jane able to leave her husband and complete a four-year degree in nursing while living in a housing project beset by drugs and crime, while Linda, on the other hand, after leaving her abuser numerous times, eventually decided that leaving presented too many obstacles and that she would have to "wait it out" until her children were older? The reasons are complex. While numerous women *leave* their abusers because of their children, others *return* to their abuser because of their children.

The court system can end up acting either like an ally or like an enemy for the battered women and children. In Linda's case, the court system did not support her efforts to protect her children, nor did the judge take into serious consideration the fact that her four-year-old had been physically abused by her batterer. Linda was charged with neglect by Social Services for remaining in the relationship, which increased her fear of becoming homeless and thus losing custody of her children. And while Social Services acknowledged that her spouse had abused the child, they did nothing on her behalf to help her seek custody.

Jane's situation reveals a different type of injustice. She was unable to afford legal representation, which would have allowed her to file for divorce and liquidation of the marital property. Public defense agencies vary from state to state, and when she sought legal help in her area, she was told that they did not accept cases concerning the division of marital property. So she and her children suffered the further injustice of having to live in a crime-infested housing project while her husband lagged behind on his child support and continued to enjoy the benefits of a quarter-million-dollar home in the suburbs.

Linda had five children, all under the age of five, while Jane had two children of junior high age. Many women who leave their abusive partners are unable to enroll their children in school because they lack proper birth and immunization records, which batterers frequently have destroyed as part of their effort to control the family.[7] When this occurs, domestic violence shelter programs act a a bridge between school officials and the children, providing documentation of abuse and assisting the battered woman in obtaining new documentation.

Libby was lucky—she was able to live with her aunt in another state, and her husband lost interest in manipulating her through the children. But what about women like Linda who are charged with neglect, even though their partners are abusing the children? Social workers need to be deeply involved in cases where domestic violence exists and to become well educated on the problem of abuse and the characteristics of the batterer and victim. Last, but not least, the faith community is vital to the overall well-being of the battered woman and her children.

NOTES

1. Bowker, Arbitell, and McFerron, "On the Relationship Between Wife Beating and Child Abuse," *Feminist Perspectives on Wife Abuse,*

Kersti Yllo and Michelle Bogard, eds., Focus Edition Series (Newbury Park, Calif.: Sage Publications, Inc., 1988).

2. Murray A. Straus and Richard J. Gelles, *Physical Violence in American Families* (New Brunswick, N.J.: Transaction Publications, 1990); in NCADV fact sheet.

3. Pfout, Schopler, and Henley, "Forgotten Victims of Family Violence," in *Social Work,* July 1982.

4. Peter G. Jaffe and David A. Wolfe, edited by Susan K. Wilson, *Children of Battered Women*, Developmental Clinical Psychology and Psychiatry Series, vol. 1 (Newbury Park, Calif.: Sage Publications, Inc., 1990).

5. Barbara Hart, "Children of Domestic Violence: Risks and Remedies," *Protective Services Quarterly,* Winter 1993.

6. "Action Notes," National Coalition Against Domestic Violence, 1989.

7. Joan Zorza, "Women Battering: A Major Cause of Homelessness," *Clearinghouse Review,* Special Issue, 1991. See also Jaffe, Wolfe, and Wilson, *Children of Battered Women.*

CHAPTER SIX

How Pastors and Church Communities Can Help

There are clearly some very important things that pastors and church members can do to help in abusive situations. Understanding the importance of setting and maintaining healthy boundaries and knowing how to practice crisis intervention with the implementation of active listening skills can make a positive difference in the life of the victim of domestic violence.

Christian counselors, pastors, and members of the faith community can share the love of Christ with the woman in crisis. The right kind of comfort is invaluable, and appropriate nurturing can help the abused individual to gain strength and confidence. God calls us as children of the light to show compassion to the wounded.

Setting Healthy Boundaries in Counseling Battered Women

Battered women sometimes find it difficult to make choices, mainly because someone else has always made the big decisions in their lives. Many women who live in violent homes went from their father's house straight into their abuser's house, never experiencing the opportunity to make their own personal choices. For this reason, it is important that you encourage her to think for herself about the various options available to her. Avoid saying "I'll take care of everything for you," and do not make all of her phone calls for her.

Point her in the right direction and make certain that she has a safe place, but do not fall into the rescuer role. This will not help her ultimately—and it will not be emotionally or spiritually healthy for you, either.

Do, however, make it clear that you will support her, pray for her, and be there for her no matter what she decides to do. This does not mean that you will reinforce any denial on her part regarding the abuse, which is apt to continue if she remains with her partner. It simply means that you will not be judgmental regarding her decisions.

To set and maintain healthy boundaries:

• Avoid falling into the rescuer role. She needs to feel empowered, not helpless. Tell her that you can guide her on spiritual matters but are not trained to deal with her situation. At the same time, strongly encourage her to obtain the information she needs to protect herself and to seek advocacy from an agency that specializes in domestic violence issues.

• Make it clear from the beginning what you can and cannot do to help. For example, you will not turn your back on her if she refuses to seek support and advocacy from a domestic violence agency. However, you cannot be called on in the middle of the night to break up a fight. This is the responsibility of local law enforcement.

• If she agrees to seek assistance from a domestic violence agency, ask her to sign a release form allowing you to discuss pertinent issues with her caseworker.

• Know that you cannot make the violence disappear or change her batterer's abusive behavior patterns. You can, however, make her abuser step down from any leadership positions that he is holding within your church and encourage him to enter into a batterer's treatment program.

A Word about Couples Counseling

When counseling a couple within your congregation, it is important that you interview them separately. Appropriate screening is crucial and should include questions regarding family history and domestic violence. If you discover that violence is occurring, you should immediately refer the woman to someone who is specifically trained in the issues of domestic violence. Your local shelter program for battered women should be able to make the appropriate referrals. Mental health professionals are not always trained in crisis intervention methods for battered women mainly because battering is not considered to be a psychological problem but a social issue. For this reason, many psychologists work in conjunction with domestic violence professionals, referring their clients to shelter staff for additional counseling and legal advocacy.

Never attempt to counsel a couple together if there is violence within the relationship. Unless the abuse has totally stopped for many years and the abuser has completed a program designed specifically for batterers, couples counseling will only serve to increase the risk of danger to the woman. This is because battering is a control issue and not a communication issue, and couples counseling poses a major threat to the abuser's control over the relationship. In order for couples counseling to be effective, equality is needed between the partners involved. Unfortunately, when the dark veil of violence hovers over a relationship, there can be no equality in the communication process during the sessions because the woman will fear future retaliation for her honesty. This not only makes the marital counseling process ineffective; it also places her life at risk.

Unfortunately, despite the fact that the National Coalition Against Domestic Violence speaks out strongly against couples counseling, many professional counselors and pastors continue to engage in it.

General Guidelines for Counseling the Battered Woman

A battered woman in the midst of a crisis is at a critical place in her life. When offered a listening ear and concrete resources, she can become much stronger and go forward with a workable plan. When sent away empty, she may not survive.

Your resource file should include the telephone number of the local domestic violence program in your area (and some of their business cards if possible), along with names and telephone numbers of individuals within the church and community who specialize in domestic violence. It is also a good idea to have a variety of books available in your church library on the topic of domestic violence. When a battered woman seeks your help, provide her with a small business card that contains the crisis line of your nearest domestic violence program. You might even want to write a reassuring Scripture on the back of the card. The card should be small enough for her to hide inside her billfold or shoe.

Here are some overall guidelines for pastors, counselors, and laity who find themselves counseling a battered woman:

Do:

• Refer the woman to your local domestic violence program for support, advocacy, and possible shelter. If there isn't a shelter nearby, pay for her to stay at a motel until you can get her admitted into a shelter within your state. (In the near future, investigate the possibility of having a shelter established in your community.)

• Tell her that she does not deserve to be abused.

• Acknowledge the seriousness of her situation and validate her experience.

• Affirm that it is difficult to discuss interpersonal problems, assure her of your nonjudgmental support, and commend her for her courage.

• Assure her that her sharing is confidential and that you will not tell her partner that she sought your help.

• Use active listening skills (see "Developing Active Listening Skills," page 61).

• Ask her if the abuse is currently occurring and, if so, proceed to assist (see "Crisis Intervention," page 52).

Do not:

• Assume the role of primary counselor when assisting the battered woman.

• Make excuses for her abusive partner.

• Tell her that she should submit to her abuser.

• Tell her that she should not do anything to "set him off."

- Tell her that she needs to see a therapist. (Remember, she is the victim, not the perpetrator.)
- Tell her that it is God's will for her to be abused.

Crisis Intervention

When assisting the woman in crisis, it is important that you ask her certain questions regarding the pattern of abuse and help her identify which stage of abuse she is in (see chapter 4). More than likely, she will not be aware of the three stages listed, but when you point them out to her, she will recognize each one.

Ask her to describe the circumstances of the last two or three beatings. What is his preabusive behavior like? Does she have some warning signs from her partner before the abuse begins? Does he begin using drugs or alcohol prior to an abusive outbreak? Does his faultfinding increase just before an onset of violence? What about his religious tendencies? Does her abuser become more fanatical just prior to a violent attack? Does he make her sit for hours while he preaches to her regarding her bad behavior as a wife and mother?

Helping her develop a clearer awareness of these patterns will assist in securing her safety. If you see a pattern, ask her if she feels that your observation is accurate. If she is able to identify stage one of her abuser's pattern, she will generally have a good idea of how long stage one lasts before he moves into the second, most dangerous, stage. If his pattern is to beat her over a period of several days, and she has already received one beating before arriving at your office, she should seek temporary refuge. If there has been a long "honeymoon" period and she senses from his preabusive behavior that it is about to end, she will probably have time to plan an emergency exit (see Appendix B) before the onset of another beating.

If a woman in crisis calls you and expresses fear of her abuser, quickly ask her the following questions:

- Are you being abused now? Is your partner there with you? If the answer to both questions is yes, then tell her to hang up and call the police. Tell her to request that they take her to a safe place and ask her to call you again after she has arrived there. Be sure that you have her correct street address so that you can also call the police and alert them to the situation. If there is no room for her at the battered women's shelter, arrange for her to stay at a motel for the night at your church's expense. Or call a caring church member who has already agreed to help a battered woman in an emergency.

• If she is not presently being abused but has received a threatening call from her abuser stating that he is planning to hurt her or kill her when he gets home, ask her if she has transportation. If the answer is yes, then she should leave without delay and go to a friend's house or shelter or wherever she knows of a safe place. You may need to help her quickly decide where to go. Is there a willing family in your church who would shelter her until other arrangements can be made? If she has no transportation, then she should seek shelter at a neighbor's house and call you from there. Meanwhile, contact the local domestic violence program for back-up. If the above options are not possible, proceed by calling a taxi for her to take to a designated "safety zone."

• Ask her if she has an emergency exit package prepared to take with her (see Appendix B). If not, suggest that, if she has time, she pack a complete change of clothing for herself (and her children)— including nightgowns, coats or sweaters, and shoes and socks, house keys, money, prescribed medications, and diapers and toys if necessary. If she has no time to pack, assure her that she can retrieve these items later. Escaping with her life is top priority.

If the woman in crisis arrives at your office with injuries from a recent beating:

• Arrange for her to receive immediate medical attention at either a hospital or doctor's office, depending on her injuries.

• Call the domestic violence program in your area and ask for a staff person or trained volunteer to meet her at the hospital or doctor's office.

Chronic Problems

Is she receiving hang-up calls from her abuser?

• Suggest that she contact her telephone company to find out about call-tracing or call-return features.

- Suggest that she get an unlisted number.

Does she think she is being stalked by her abuser?

- Give her the number of the local legal-aid services.

- Encourage her to write down times, locations, and dates of the incidents. The majority of battered women complain of being stalked when they try to leave an abusive partner. An abuser may try to find the woman and harass her, reasoning that if she loses her job, she will return to him. The definition of stalking includes following or being in the presence of another without legal purpose and with the intent of causing emotional distress by creating fear of bodily harm. Other components that must be present include a warning to desist by or on behalf of the other person and evidence of a pattern of such behavior.

Is fear keeping her from sleeping?

- Have her write down her worst fears. Then help her sort through what is and is not reasonable. For example, does she fear that God will severely punish her for leaving the violent home? This is not a reasonable fear. Allow her to help decide which fears are unmerited. Don't forget that the batterer has tremendous power over the battered woman, at least in her own mind, and this includes her perception of God. He may have threatened to pray for her demise if she dared to leave him. Reassure her of God's unconditional love for her.

- Does she fear that her abuser will follow her home from her place of employment? This is a reasonable fear. Help her design safety precautions. For example, can she stagger her working hours so that he will not know her routine? Can she hide her car or ride to work with a friend? Helping the battered woman manage her fears puts her back in control of her life.

- Give her empowering verses of Scripture to have with her at all times, such as Psalm 34:4: "I sought the LORD, and he answered me, and delivered me from all my fears."

Other Practical Ways to Help Battered Women

- Establish an emergency fund for victims of domestic violence. Use this money to meet the needs of battered women in your church and community. These funds could be used to pay rental deposits or electric bills for women who are struggling to make it on their own. They could also be used for sheltering women in motels when a room is not available in a shelter.

• Seek out sensitive individuals from the congregation and request their assistance in providing back-up for women in crisis situations. Women who have healed from domestic violence often discover their own previously unknown strengths and skills by helping other women. Once recovered from the nightmare of abuse, they can open up and be helpful to others who are experiencing the same traumatic issues. Survivors of domestic violence make wonderful volunteers for shelter programs, and they generally seem to have a good and strong intuition, more than likely developed through the pain of their own experiences. The most courageous and helpful people have frequently had hurtful experiences that have fine-tuned their compassion toward those who are in pain. Encourage them, if they are ready and willing, to use their gifts and past experiences to help others in need.

• Take the time to visit your local battered women's shelter and get acquainted with its staff members.

• Invite a staff member of your local domestic violence program to offer training sessions to members of your church who are interested in helping. Most shelter programs require their volunteers to complete a specific number of hours in training. Take the time to receive the necessary training so that you, and all church members who want to help, will be prepared to assist women in crisis.

• If there is not a shelter for battered women in your area, consider helping to create one. Remember, many homeless shelters will not accept women at all, and those that do frequently turn away battered women since their abusers pose a threat to the safety of the other residents. Shelters for battered women are much needed and are a wonderful ministry for churches.

Domestic violence programs have brought significant aid to many abused women and are supported by a diverse group of organizations across the country. This surge of support for domestic violence programs by all sectors is astonishing. Perhaps it is because battering affects not only the victimized woman but also society as a whole; we as a society bear an inordinate penalty for what happens in the home. Numerous battered women are physically and emotionally unable to support themselves and must receive welfare, Medicaid, and public legal services. Statistics clearly reveal that incidents of violence in the home far outnumber the frequency of other violent crimes and are often the precursor to other types of violence. Thus it is crucial that prevention and intervention are taught and practiced by everyone who is touched by this epidemic.

How to Handle the Batterer

All of us can recall moving testimonies from former drug addicts, alcoholics, and even hardened criminals who became productive citizens after turning their lives over to Christ. Why is it that we are not hearing similar testimonies from "former batterers"? Might it be because the church has sanctioned family violence by its silence on the issue?

The first thing that pastors and congregations can do is to break the silence. This will let both victims and perpetrators know that others are aware of the "hidden" problem of domestic violence. Pastors and members of the Christian community can learn about the problem of battering and how to respond by reading books such as this and by contacting their local battered women's shelter and the organizations listed in Appendix A for more information.

Next, holding batterers responsible for their actions should be top priority within the Christian community. Intervention based on confrontation and tough love is the prerequisite for change. I firmly believe that if abusers are confronted and faced with tangible consequences within their place of worship, we as a society would witness a dramatic drop in violent crimes against women.

But no matter how many programs are implemented within the church and community, the abuser must accept personal responsibility for his violence before any treatment can be successful. True change requires the courage and willingness to think and act differently. As Christians, we know that we do not have to do anything to earn God's love and forgiveness, but if we are to grow spiritually, we are required to practice our faith and develop our spiritual gifts. While we cannot help what we feel, we are all free to choose how we act on our feelings.

Identifying the Potential Batterer

It is important that pastors, counselors, and Christian friends remember that seemingly "nice guys" can abuse their wives—and most batterers do not go to their pastors for help. The following checklist can help pastors and others in the church community determine the presence of abusive and violent behavior in their midst. It can be used with either the husband (to check what he has done) or the wife (to check what has been done to her):

- Does he isolate her, making it difficult for her to see family or friends?
- Does he use intimidation tactics, such as standing over her or preventing her from leaving the room?
- Does he engage in uninvited touching or use coercion to obtain sex?
- Does he give harsh personal criticism, including name calling and put-downs?
- Does he use pressure tactics to control her, including threats to withhold financial support?
- Does he sabotage her attempts to work outside the home?
- Does he cause problems at her workplace?
- Does he twist her words?
- Does he manipulate the children?
- Does he claim the "truth" by defining and analyzing her behavior?
- Does he claim absolute authority?
- Does he make uninvited visits or calls after separation?
- Does he publicly embarrass her?
- Does he drive recklessly?
- Does he use weapons against her (or *threaten* to use them)?

Responding Biblically to the Batterer

Batterers often frequent churches both during and after episodes of violence. Unfortunately, churches often provide a good facade for the abuser and are relatively easy places in which he can affirm his image as a good, religious man and further intimidate his victim. Women who escape from battering situations may be stalked at church, as well as telephoned and otherwise harassed by their partners, for quite some time after separation.

Theresa tried to attend church after leaving her abuser, but she found that each Sunday he was waiting for her in the sanctuary. "I didn't want to make a scene right there in church, but that's exactly what he wanted me to do," she said. "I would find little notes from him in my Bible telling me that he still loved me and that I needed to forgive him and come back home."

All Theresa wanted to do was go to church and worship, but her abuser made this an impossibility. "He would tell me that he had asked God to forgive him and that the ball was now in my court, that it was my place to forgive and take him back. What a guilt trip that put me on! Finally, when I realized that my pastor would not ask him to stop coming to church and annoying me, I stopped going there. It just wasn't worth the hassle."

Pastors should be sensitive to the feelings of battered women who wish to attend church but cannot do so because of an abuser's constant harassment. Theresa is not the first battered woman who tried to return to church only to find her abuser waiting for her each Sunday morning. Unfortunately, the woman is usually the one who gives up her place of worship because it is likely that no one in leadership will tell the batterer to leave. Debra, for example, attended church most of the time during her marriage. Her husband was never very involved. But after the relationship dissolved, Debra's ex-husband was at every function. When she consulted her pastor about the matter, he told her that her abuser was just as welcome as anyone else in God's house. On the surface this may sound reasonable, loving, and biblical. But does Scripture give any specific guidance concerning batterers other than to love and accept them?

Yes! Consider Christ's detailed instruction on confronting "offenders" within the church (Matthew 18:15-17). According to Jesus, the offender should be confronted privately at first. If he does not listen, the pastor should take one or two other church leaders along to discuss the problem. If that course of action does not work, then the matter should be taken before the entire church. If the offender still does not listen, he should be treated as a pagan or tax collector. Being treated as a pagan or tax collector was not exactly a compliment during the time of our Lord! But Jesus, in all his mercy and kindness, indicated that at times certain people should be excluded from some communities of worship.

I believe that telling the abuser to leave the congregation and to worship elsewhere is the only spiritually and scripturally correct thing to do. It shows batterers that violence will not be tolerated by the faith community—and allows battered women and their children to worship in peace and regain their trust in a loving God.

At the very least, known or suspected batterers should not be allowed to hold leadership positions in the church. If a church member were to assault a stranger, commit murder, or rob a bank, he would be urged by his pastor to turn himself in to the police. If this same individual held a leadership position within the congregation, he would be forced to step down until the matter was resolved. But when a man within the Christian community breaks the law by battering his wife, he is seldom asked to step down from leadership or leave the church. Instead, more often than not, his wife is even blamed, directly or indirectly, for the violence.

According to 1 Timothy 3:2-5, however, church leaders should be *sober, self-controlled, nonviolent, gentle, and peaceful.* They should be capable of managing their own families and should be respected by their children. Managing one's household certainly does not mean controlling and terrorizing the entire family! Instead, in Galatians 5:22-25 we read that the Holy Spirit has given the Christian new life and is to be our guide and bring forth good fruit, including *kindness, gentleness, and self-control.* When one's life is controlled by the Holy Spirit, there will be *self*-control, not seeking to control another individual.

Many within the faith community believe that husbands should be the "head of the home," making all of the big decisions and accepting full responsibility for their failures, while wives are to be "submissive" to their husbands. The issue of submission remains a volatile subject, and Christians from all denominations express a variety of opinions on the matter. Frequently, the battering husband will boast of his role as "head of the home" while he controls and abuses his wife and children.

Regardless of how one interprets the Scripture on submission (Ephesians 5:21-33), nothing in the text encourages or supports physical violence. In fact, the Scripture might even imply that women who are battered by their husbands are released from their marriage vows, as it clearly states that men should love their wives as Christ loved the church and gave his life for her (v. 25). In the same way, a husband should be willing to die for his wife—not attempt to take life from her, as the batterer attempts to do. The Christlike man will treat his partner with tenderness and respect and will encourage her to develop the gifts that God has given her. He will not become jealous of her accomplishments or other friendships, for he will view her successes as an extension of their relationship.

General Guidelines for Counseling the Batterer

If you find yourself counseling or confronting a batterer, the following general guidelines should be followed:

• Refer the abuser to a batterers' treatment program in your area, if one exists. If there is none, contact your local mental health association or Men Stopping Violence, Inc.; 1020 Dekalb Avenue, #25; Atlanta, GA 30307 (phone: 404-688-1376) for information.

• Do not believe excuses such as "She drove me to it" or patronizing statements such as "I did it for her own good."

• Be direct. Tell him that he needs help and that his violent behavior is wrong.

• Do not allow a batterer to hold leadership positions within the church.

• Make every effort to get him to leave the house. Suggest that he allow himself time to cool down. Tell him that you want to help him but that "family safety first" is the rule that is to be followed.

Other Practical Ways to Deal with Batterers

• Visit the local batterers' treatment program if one exists and learn more.

• Ask an expert for advice on how to deal with abusive men.

• Invite someone from the batterers' treatment program to visit your church and speak with the entire congregation regarding the problem of battering.

• Form a men's support group and encourage all men within the church to attend. Offer information obtained from batterers' treatment programs, including studies on such issues as the need to control the behavior of others and emphasizing the sinful and criminal nature of violent acts.

• Don't wear blinders! Abusive men are in all churches, and many of them are ones that you would least suspect.

Developing Active Listening Skills

In active listening, the "listener" reflects back what he or she has heard the other person say. The active listener may occasionally insert a nonjudgmental comment or reassurance. Comments should be restricted to ones that pertain only to a battered woman's personal safety and self-esteem. For example, telling the woman that she is in stage two of the cycle of abuse is an opinion pertaining to her safety. An unacceptable opinion on the part of an active listener would be, "You're crazy for staying with this guy!" Inappropriate opinions place the active listener in a judgmental role, which leaves the victim feeling even more powerless.

The "sender," the woman in crisis in our case, then verifies whether the listener has heard correctly. In cases of domestic abuse, listeners need to make every effort to understand what the "sender" is saying and feeling. When listening:

Do:

• Stay alert and attentive. Don't stare out the window or check your watch.

• Allow her to do most of the talking, especially during the first few minutes, inserting noncommittal acknowledgment words such as "yes," "uh-huh," "I see," and "I understand" so that she knows she is being heard.

• Use empowering words and statements such as "You deserve

a life that is free of abuse!" and "Your church is here for you, no matter what you choose to do."

Do not:

• Direct, order, or command her. Avoid statements such as, "If you want the violence to stop, then you must . . ."
• Cross-examine her with questions such as, "What is the reason for . . .?" and "But earlier on you said . . ."
• Diagnose and analyze her. Don't say, "Your *real* problem is . . ."
• Offer false reassurances such as "Don't worry about a thing— everything is going to be just fine" or "He's just saying these things to scare you. He really doesn't mean it."
• Make admonishing statements like, "I'll help you this time, but if you go back to him, I will no longer be here for you."

The following discussion illustrates how, through active listening, a pastor, counselor, or friends can help a woman in crisis better understand herself and her situation and become empowered to begin finding solutions:

Woman in crisis: "For a time my husband was doing fine. Now he seems to be getting worse. I try to be a good wife to him, but the least little thing that I do sets him off these days."

Active listener: "You feel that the violence is getting worse?"

Woman in crisis: "Oh, yes, it's much worse. Last night he held me against the gas range, almost burning my face. He said it was because I had overcooked his steak. Holding my face near the flame was supposed to show me how hot it was—it was to show me that if I had been paying closer attention to the temperature setting, I would not have accidentally overcooked his food."

Active listener: "You must have been afraid!"

Woman in crisis: "I didn't mean to burn his supper—it didn't look ruined! He always liked his steaks well done before. I guess I really wasn't paying much attention, but he shouldn't have held me over the stove."

Active listener: "There's never any excuse for violence, and he should not have held you over the stove!"

Woman in crisis: "I never quite know from one day to the next what he expects. He wants our home to be perfect, but his definition of perfection changes from one day to the next. And he has never forgiven me for the loss of our baby."

She begins to cry. At this point the active listener should offer her a tissue and give her a moment to collect herself. Tell her it is safe to cry in your presence. Many battered women are told by their abusive partners that they are not to cry under any circumstances. Offer her a cup of coffee or tea or a glass of water. Allow adequate time for her to collect her thoughts. Don't rush her, but at the same time, help her to refocus and gain control. Most battered women live in extreme circumstances of good and bad. Giving her room to freely express her feelings and then helping her to refocus is good advocacy procedure.

Active listener: "You mentioned losing your baby?"

Woman in crisis: "Yes, he holds that against me even though I almost fell apart when it happened. If I had it to do all over again, things would be different. But I can't turn back the hands of time, can I?"

Active listener: "How old was the baby?"

Woman in crisis: "I was three months pregnant when I had the miscarriage. I smoked cigarettes during the first four weeks of my pregnancy, but I immediately stopped when I discovered that I was pregnant. My husband insists that my smoking killed our unborn child, that I deliberately murdered our baby just to hurt him! But I really wanted the baby! He was the one who took the news of my pregnancy so badly! In fact, on the evening that I announced to him that I was expecting, he told me that we could not afford another mouth to feed and that I had allowed myself to become pregnant just to put him deeper in debt. 'What debt?' I asked him. I knew that he had been stashing every penny he made in the bank for the previous two years while we lived on the money that I made as a teacher. My question made him so angry that he cornered me against the wall and began punching me over and over again in the stomach. When I began having severe cramps, I begged him to take me to the hospital, but he just laughed and told me that I had gotten exactly what I deserved. After he fell asleep, I called my mother, and she took me to the hospital."

Active listener: "And you miscarried that night?"

Woman in crisis: "Yes, six hours later. The next day he came to the hospital with a bouquet of roses telling me that all was forgiven. He promised to never hit me again—but still insisted that smoking had caused me to lose the baby. He told me that the doctor had confirmed his suspicions regarding my miscarriage."

Active listener: "And did you talk with your doctor regarding the matter?"

Woman in crisis: "Yes, I asked if smoking could cause a miscarriage, and he said that it was possible but more likely it was my husband's abuse that had caused me to lose the baby."

Active listener: "But you still blame yourself? Even though the doctor confirmed that your husband's abuse probably caused you to miscarry?"

Woman in crisis: "I suppose I do. But on the other hand, it seems foolish of me to believe such a thing. To tell you the truth, I'm not sure what to believe anymore."

Active listener: "It sounds as though you're a little confused about what to believe and what not to believe."

Woman in crisis: "It's just that I feel I must agree with him all the time, just to keep down problems. If he speaks badly about a neighbor and I disagree with him, he accuses me of having an affair with the neighbor! But if I agree with him about the neighbor, hoping to prevent an argument, he will tell me I am not capable of thinking on my own, accuse me of being stupid, and then beat me anyway. Either way, whether I agree or disagree, I usually get it. If he says the sofa is blue, but I know that the sofa is really green, I'll agree with him, hoping to escape his wrath. Sometimes this tactic works—sometimes it does not. I suppose that's why I don't know what to believe anymore."

Active listener: "Maybe you're not as confused as you think. If I'm hearing you right, and please correct me if I'm not, you already know that the sofa is green and not blue, but you agree with this man in order to try to protect yourself. That sounds like a good survival tactic. What do you think?"

Woman in crisis: "Well, yes. I never thought of it quite like that before. I suppose I am just trying to survive. I do still know the difference between right and wrong ... Maybe there is a difference, as you say, between confusion and survival. They sometimes feel the same, but they're different."

Active listener: "And you knew that you needed to go to the hospital immediately after a severe beating—and you were focused enough to pick up the phone and call your mother. Moreover, you were thinking clearly enough, even though you were in pain, to wait until he was asleep before making that phone call. Those are survival skills."

Woman in crisis: "Yes, that's true! Thank you for helping me see that. He's always telling me I'm crazy. Last night, when he shoved me into the range, he told me I was too crazy to teach school full-time. He only allows me to substitute and, although I fill in three or four days per week for teachers who are sick, I don't have my own class of children to work with—so a bond is never really formed."

Active listener: "What would happen if you decided to take a full-time position?"

Woman in crisis: "Oh, he wouldn't allow that! Last night, after he almost burned my face, he shoved me against the wall and told me I wouldn't be so lucky next time. This scares me. In fact, I'm too frightened to even dream of taking a full-time position."

Active listener: "It sounds as though you are in the second phase of the abuse cycle, which is the most dangerous time for women who have violent partners. I think it would be a really good idea for you to leave home, at least until he has had a chance to cool off. Let me give you the number of the shelter for battered women. They can help."

Woman in crisis: "Oh, I'm not sure—the last time I left him he was really mad! I went to my mother's house, and he harassed her at work and almost caused her to lose her job! I finally went back to him because he promised to never hit me again—but at the same time, he told me he would kill not only me but my entire family if I ever tried to leave him again."

Active listener: "The shelter for battered women can help you in many ways that I can't. They can provide legal advocacy and information, as well as total anonymity so that your husband won't know where to find you."

Woman in crisis: "But I'm so scared of strange new places . . . How would God feel about my getting a divorce? I'd be breaking my marriage vows, wouldn't I?"

Active listener: "I don't really think that divorce is an issue right now. We can discuss that topic later on, if you like, but for the moment I am genuinely concerned for your safety. And I can tell you that it is not God's will for men to abuse their wives and place their lives at risk."

Woman in crisis: "Oh, if only he would change! He can be such a good and wonderful man when he is not hurting me. Couldn't you talk to him? Couldn't you tell him what you just told me about it not being God's will for men to abuse their wives? Maybe that would make him stop."

Active listener: "Of course, I'd be happy to talk with him, but only if you are out of harm's way. I could suggest that he enter into a batterers' treatment program, and if he chooses to do so, and continues to participate in the program's after-care procedures, I'd be happy to offer him spiritual guidance. But for the moment, I think that we must work on designing a plan for your personal safety."

Woman in crisis: "Okay—but I feel like such a failure."

Active listener: "You're not a failure. You're a valuable person. You are a child of God."

If she continues to express that she loves her abuser and does not want her marriage to end, try to keep her directed toward her personal safety. Most women do not want their relationship to dissolve—they just want the violence to end. Emphasize to her that seeking temporary shelter does not mean the marriage is over. She can make those decisions later. Stress the importance of seeking refuge while the abuser is in the violent stage. This tactic may save her life.

The woman in crisis may be concerned about her abuser finding out about her visit with you, and thus be worried about physical retaliation. Assure her that everything she says, along with the fact that she is seeking your help, will be held in strictest confidence. She may also be concerned that she will be pressured into filing for divorce or pressing criminal charges. The battered woman must be assured that her needs will be met as *she* defines them. As her pastor, let her know that you are there to offer spiritual guidance and to pray for her as well as to encourage her to seek personal safety.

A Time for Action

It may be hard for us to imagine that any men in our midst abuse their wives or that what a woman is telling us about her husband's violence toward her is true. But battering is a widespread problem, and very few women make up such stories. So we must listen and take them seriously, as not only their (and their children's) physical and emotional safety are at stake but also their lives and their futures. Pastors, counselors, and Christian friends should never underestimate the battered woman's worst fears. Since women who are killed by their abusive partners are most often killed *after* escaping the violence, it is also important to offer assistance beyond the immediate crisis, to become familiar with the resources available for both her short-term and long-term safety, and to encourage her to take the required precautions for her security.

After you become informed about domestic violence and listen to women who are being battered, it is time to take action. Though churches and pastors may not be experts in domestic violence issues and the treatment of batterers, they can learn how to identify battered individuals and their abusers and learn to apply the appropriate intervention techniques to reduce the danger.

The faith community is to be a symbol of Christ's commitment to peace and safety for the family. It can with confidence create positive programs within the church that will heighten awareness of family violence as well as guide victims and abusers toward the necessary resources for their healing. In order to accomplish this, first the church must no longer deny the existence of the problem. It is essential that the entire congregation offers support to the woman who chooses to walk away from her abuser in order to find a nonviolent life. It is also crucial for men to confront men who are batterers and challenge them to work to overcome their violent patterns of behavior.

My prayer for today's church is that we become more receptive to the needs of the families torn apart by domestic violence. The church must decide how to use its power to positively affect the outcome of an abusive situation. Healing begins when people learn to see beyond the illusions that cover up the reality of domestic violence and open their eyes to the pain that is tearing families apart. Then Christians, as members of the mystical body of Christ, can set a constructive course to aid those who desperately need their help.

Resources
for the Battered Woman

The following list of groups is a starting point for pastors and other individuals interested in obtaining more information. While many groups are national, they will usually be able to provide you with a local referral. All (800) numbers listed are state hotlines. For further information regarding domestic violence issues, call the National Coalition Against Domestic Violence at 303-839-1852.

Advocates for Battered Women
P.O. Box 1954
Little Rock, AR 72203
(800) 332-4443 (hotline)
(501) 376-3219

American Association of Pastoral Counselors
9504A Lee Highway
Fairfax, VA 22031
(703) 385-6967

Center for Adult Survivors of Sexual Abuse
205 Avenue 1, Suite 27
Redondo Beach, CA 90277
(310) 379-5929

The Center for the Prevention of Sexual and Domestic Violence
1914 N. 34th Street, #105
Seattle, WA 98103
(800) 562-6025 (emergency)
(206) 634-1903

The Task Force on Child Abuse of the Episcopal Diocese of Los Angeles
P.O. Box 2164
1220 W. 4th Street
Los Angeles, CA 90051
(Publishers of the "Child Abuse Prevention Handbook," a manual for Episcopal churches, schools, and institutions)

Committee on the Status of Women
Women in Mission and Ministry Office
The Episcopal Church Center
815 Second Avenue
New York, NY 10017
(800) 334-7626

Men Stopping Violence
1020 Dekalb Avenue #25
Atlanta, GA 30307
(404) 688-1376

National Clearinghouse for the Defense of Battered Women
125 S. 9th Street, Suite 302
Philadelphia, PA 19107
(215) 351-0010

National Coalition Against Domestic Violence
P.O. Box 34103
Washington, DC 20043-4103
(202) 638-6388
(303) 839-1852

Center for the Prevention of Domestic Violence and Sexual Assault
1914 N. 34th Street, Suite 105
Seattle, WA 98103
(206) 634-1903
[Producers of the video "Not in My Church" (1991), available to rent from EcuFilm at (800) 251-4091]

The Safer Society Program
P.O. Box 340

Brandon, VT 05733
(802) 247-3132
(a national project of the New York State Council of Churches, which maintains a national listing of agencies and treatment programs for young and adult violent offenders and sexual-abuse victims and offenders)

U.S. Help Lines for Women

Alabama
(205) 832-4842

Alaska
(907) 586-3650

Arizona
(602) 224-9477

Arkansas
(501) 663-4668

Central California
(209) 524-1888

Northern California
(415) 457-2464

Southern California
(213) 655-6098

Colorado
(303) 573-9018

Connecticut
(203) 524-5898

Delaware
(302) 762-6110

District of Columbia
(202) 546-4996

Florida
(407) 628-3885

Georgia
(404) 524-3847

Hawaii
(808) 595-3900

Idaho
(208) 338-1323

Illinois
(217) 789-2830

Indiana
(317) 724-0075
(800) 332-7385

Iowa
(515) 281-7284

Kansas
(316) 232-2527

Kentucky
(502) 875-4132

Louisiana
(504) 523-3755

Maine
(307) 941-1194

Maryland
(301) 942-0900

Massachusetts
(617) 248-0922

Michigan
(517) 484-2924
(517) 372-4960

Minnesota
(612) 646-6177

Mississippi
(601) 436-3809

Missouri
(314) 634-4161

Montana
(406) 586-7689

Nebraska
(402) 476-6256

Nevada
(702) 746-2700
(800) 992-5757

New Hampshire
(603) 224-8893

New Jersey
(609) 584-8107
(800) 572-7233

New Mexico
(515) 526-2819

New York
(518) 432-4864
(800) 942-6906 (English)
(800) 942-6908 (Spanish)

North Carolina
(919) 490-1467

North Dakota
(701) 255-6240
(800) 472-2911

Ohio
(614) 221-1255
(614) 221-0023
(800) 934-9840

Oklahoma
(405) 557-1210
(800) 522-SAFE (7233)

Oregon
(503) 239-4486, 4487

Pennsylvania
(717) 545-6400
(800) 932-4632

Rhode Island
(401) 723-3051

South Carolina
(803) 232-1339

South Dakota
(605) 624-5311

Tennessee
(615) 327-0805

Texas
(512) 794-1133

Utah
(801) 752-4493

Vermont
(802) 223-1302

Virginia
(804) 221-0990

Washington
(206) 352-4029
(800) 562-6025

West Virginia
(304) 765-2250

Wisconsin
(608) 255-0539

Wyoming
(307) 235-2814

The Emergency Exit Kit

The battered woman should pack an "emergency exit kit" to take with her if she needs to make a quick exit. Whenever possible, she should be encouraged to plan for and pack her own kit, as her own arrangements will be best tailored to suit her particular situation and needs, and she will probably follow through on plans that she makes for herself. Preparing her emergency exit kit will give her some feeling of control over her situation, as well as make her life far more manageable should she be forced from her home quickly or in the middle of the night.

The "kit" should be simple and easy to hide. If she does not have a small suitcase, then a grocery bag or pillow slip will suffice. It should include:

- Extra cash (if at all possible).
- Bank books, social security cards (for self and children), passports, green cards, special work permits, birth certificates, children's medical and inoculation records. (Having important papers expedites emergency food-stamp applications and school transfers.)
- Medications that must be administered on a daily basis. (If not possible, most physicians will give samples of medications on request.)
- At least one complete change of clothing (daytime and nighttime wear) for self and children.
- Small notebook and pen, along with a list of important names and telephone numbers.

- Bible and devotional materials.
- Toiletries and personal hygiene products.
- Familiar toys and storybooks for any children she takes with her.

Where to Hide the Emergency Exit Kit

An individual who is in crisis is vulnerable and feels at a loss about how to help herself, so having this kit prepared and in a place where she can retrieve it safely and quickly will give her added self-confidence. Suggest that she keep this kit near an exit or any place where she can safely hide it (suggestions listed below), but also stress to her that retrieving the kit is not as important as getting out of the violence safely. A hiding place outside of the home will help increase the odds of a woman being able to get the kit when it is needed.

- At church
- At her workplace
- At the home of a trustworthy relative or friend
- In her private gym locker
- In a secret location within the home—only if none of the above will work